SPIRIT OF THE SIBERIAN TIGER
Folktales of the Russian Far East

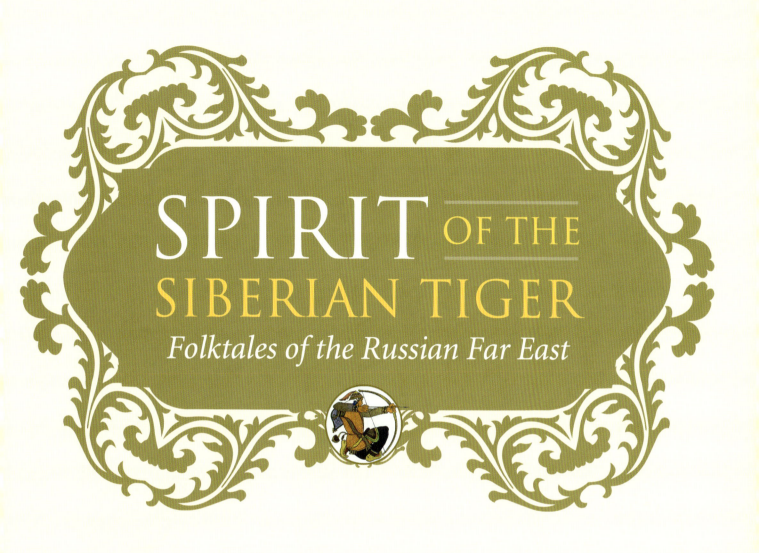

SPIRIT OF THE SIBERIAN TIGER
Folktales of the Russian Far East

To my teacher, friend, and colleague Henry N. Michael

Alexander B. Dolitsky

Edited by **Alexander B. Dolitsky**   Translated by **Henry N. Michael**

Published by Alaska-Siberia Research Center
P.O. Box 34871, Juneau, Alaska, U.S.A. 99803
www.aksrc.org
Publication No. 15

Copyright © 2008 by the Alaska-Siberia Research Center (www.aksrc.org)

All rights reserved. No part of this book may be reproduced or transmitted in any form or by any means without permission in writing from the copyright holder: Alaska-Siberia Research Center, P.O. Box 34871, Juneau, Alaska, U.S.A. 99803.

First Edition
Published by the Alaska-Siberia Research Center, P. O. Box 34871, Juneau, Alaska, U.S.A. 99803.
www.aksrc.org

Jacket illustrations by *Gennadiy Pavlishin*
Jacket oil painting on canvas by *Jason Morgan*

Printed and bound by Amica, Inc.
Printed in China

Production Manager: *Alexander B. Dolitsky*
General Editor: *Alexander B. Dolitsky*
Translator: *Henry N. Michael, Ph.D. in Anthropology/Geography*
Author of the folktales: *Dmitriy Nagishkin*
Illustrator of the folktales: *Gennadiy Pavlishin*
Book designer: *Lightbourne, Inc.*
Jacket designer: *Lightbourne, Inc.*
General Copy Editor: *Liz Dodd, IDTC*
Copy Editors: *Luke Bartlett Weld, Ph.D. in English; Kathy Kolkhorst Ruddy*
Consultants: *Willis D. Longyear, Miriam J. Lancaster, Wallace M. Olson*
Cartographer: *Brad Slama, Slama Design, Inc.*
Tiger oil paintings on canvas: *Jason Morgan*

Hardback edition ISBN 978-0-9653891-7-4
Key words: Tiger, Siberia, Amur, Folktales, Conservation

The paper in this book meets the guidelines for permanence and durability of the Committee on Production Guidelines for Book Longevity of the Council on Library Resources.

From the beginnings of human life, animals have shared our universe. Their bodies have provided food, clothing, shelter, and tools, and many traditional religions assert that their spirits continue to sustain human endeavors.

Mary Jane Lenz
National Museum of the American Indian, 2004
Smithsonian Institution, Washington, D.C.

CONTENTS

Transliteration Table viii
Preface by Alexander B. Dolitsky ix
Foreword by Wallace M. Olson xi

Introduction by Alexander B. Dolitsky 1
Ethnographic Information by Alexander B. Dolitsky ... 5
About the Siberian Tiger by Alexander B. Dolitsky ... 9
The Tyger by William Blake 13
Tiger Tiger Revisited by Gordon J.L. Ramel 15

Literary Folktales:
    The Seven Fears (Udegey) by Dmitriy Nagishkin 17
    The Little Girl Elga (Udegey) by Dmitriy Nagishkin 29
    The Greedy Kanchuga (Udegey) by Dmitriy Nagishkin ... 39
    Kile Bamba and Loche-The Strongman (Nanay) by Dmitriy Nagishkin ... 47

Suggested Bibliography 63
Glossary 65
About the Editor 67
About the Translator 69
Contributors 71
Index 73

TRANSLITERATION TABLE

The system of transliteration adopted in this work is that of the United States Board of Geographic Names with slight modifications for technical reasons. Instead of e, we use ye at the beginning of names, after vowels and after the soft sign (ь), or yo (ё) where e is accented as ё. The soft sign (ь) and hard sign (ъ) have no sound value but they soften or harden the sound of the letter in front of them. A hard sign (ъ) is transliterated when in the middle of a word and disregarded when final.

Russian Letters		Transliteration	
А	а	a	(as in star, car, Arkansas)
Б	б	b	(as in boots, Bill, Britain)
В	в	v	(as in voice, Virginia)
Г	г	g	(as in go, good, Michigan)
Д	д	d	(as in do, road, Dakota)
Е	е	ye	(as in met, yes)
Ё	ё	yo	(as in yonder, York)
Ж	ж	zh	(as in pleasure)
З	з	z	(as in zoo, is, Kansas)
И	и	i	(as in meet, seat)
Й	й	y	(as in may, boy)
К	к	k	(as in cat, kind, Kentucky)
Л	л	l	(as in belt, lion, Florida)
М	м	m	(as in amuse, mother, Mexico)
Н	н	n	(as in now, noose, Nebraska)
О	о	o	(as in port, comb, Oklahoma)
П	п	p	(as in pure, poor, Portland)
Р	р	r	(as in river, trilled, Arizona)
С	с	s	(as in swim, SOS, South)
Т	т	t	(as in stool, tiger, Texas)
У	у	u	(as in lunar, tune)
Ф	ф	f	(as in food, funny, California)
Х	х	kh	(as in Loch Ness)
Ц	ц	ts	(as in its, quartz, waltz)
Ч	ч	ch	(as in cheap, chain, cheese)
Ш	ш	sh	(as in fish, sheep, shrimp)
Щ	щ	shch	(as in borshch)
Ъ	ъ	"	(hard sign; no equivalent)
Ы	ы	y	(as in rip, flip)
Ь	ь	'	(soft sign; no equivalent)
Э	э	e	(as in best, chest, effort)
Ю	ю	yu	(as in you, Yukon)
Я	я	ya	(as in yard, yahoo)

PREFACE

This edition translates and edits four folktales from Russian into English. All four tales come from the indigenous people of the Russian Far East. Dr. Henry N. Michael translated the folktales into English from the *Amurskiye Skazki* (*Fairy Tales of the Amur*); in translating and editing the texts from Russian into English, Michael and Dolitsky have sought to preserve the specific traits of the language without violating its grammatical and stylistic norms, or the narrators' tone, style, beliefs, and oral conventions.

The Russian edition of this work was written by Dmitriy Nagishkin and illustrated by Gennadiy Pavlishin (1980).[1] Altogether, Nagishkin's Russian edition consists of thirty-one literary folktales based on and derived from the Nanay, Nivkhi, Ulchi, Udegey, Orochi, Negidal, and Orok cultural traditions and oral narratives. For this edition, Dolitsky and Michael have selected four of Nagishkin's folktales in which the Siberian tiger is closely associated with the main characters.

The Siberian tiger is a native species of the southeastern region of the Russian Far East, and an essential neighbor of the aboriginal people. Sharing the same land with the tiger for many generations, Native inhabitants of the region came to recognize the tiger's dominant presence among wildlife. The tiger is admired for its strength and agility, and feared for its ferociousness. As a central figure in their culture and everyday life, the Siberian tiger is viewed by Natives as an integral part of their universe, belief systems, and code of behavior.

The rationale for selecting folktales featuring the Siberian tiger is to alert the reader to the declining numbers of this species in its natural and historic habitat, to call for continuing preservation of this fascinating animal, and to educate those interested in folktales of the aboriginal peoples of the Russian Far East.

For their useful comments and constructive suggestions, I would like to express my thanks to consultants Professor of Anthropology Wallace M. Olson, Miriam J. Lancaster, and Willis D. Longyear; board members of the Alaska-Siberia Research Center William G. Ruddy, Robert Price, Dr. Jeffrey Hahn, Miriam J. Lancaster, and Mead Treadwell; and copy editors Dr. Luke B. Weld, Liz Dodd, and Kathy Kolkhorst Ruddy. I also wish to thank cartographer Brad Slama for his maps; Lightbourne, Inc., for designing the book and dust jacket; photographer John Gomes for providing the original photos of the Siberian tiger; and artist Jason Morgan for providing tiger images from his oil paintings.

Alexander B. Dolitsky
Alaska-Siberia Research Center

---

1 Dmitriy Nagishkin, *Amurskiye Skazki* [*Fairy Tales of the Amur*]. Khabarovsk: Khabarovsk Press, 1980.

FOREWORD

For many generations, our ancestors survived by hunting, fishing, and gathering the animals and plants around them. They possessed an intimate, detailed knowledge of their environment, seeing themselves as inseparable from the surrounding natural world. The earliest human pictographs, petroglyphs, hieroglyphs, drawings, paintings, and other symbolic representations and objects depict not just humans, but the animals and landscapes that they knew so well.

The Latin term *anima* means spirit, or soul. Early men came to believe that, like humans, all animals had a spirit and an inner being that kept them alive. Today, the term *animism* is used to describe this belief system. These beliefs extended not just to large animals, such as the mammoth, the bear, or the tiger, but also to a wide range of apparently very clever or enigmatic creatures, like ravens, coyotes, frogs, beavers, eagles, and butterflies; and to physical features today considered "inanimate," such as glaciers.

The ancient stories, then, talk not only about the individual physical beings, but about their spirits as well. Orally transmitted tales speak of the great spirits—Raven, Eagle, Bear, Tiger, and many others. At times, these spirits could change from their normal physical form and take on human form, while communicating and interacting with humans. People and animals shared a spirit world.

We humans spend almost a third of our lives sleeping and, at times, dreaming. In dreams, people travel to strange places, fly through space, speak with the deceased, engage in elaborate adventures, and temporarily live the spirit life. Some individuals are thought to have the ability to understand and interpret these dreams. In oral narratives of Siberian people, these individuals are known by various local terms. Anthropologists refer to them as *shamans*, or "medicine men,"[2] because with their knowledge they can cure the spiritual ills of others, or interpret events with an adequate level of accuracy. Traditional folktales reflect this relationship between everyday life and the *animistic-shamanistic* spiritual experience.

---

[2] Editor's note: *Shamanism*, a symbolic system of beliefs, is associated with religious practices first observed at the end of the seventeenth century among the Natives of Siberia. *Shamanic* rituals enact, as if on a stage, the complex relationships of exchange and interdependency between the people and their game animals. *Shamanism* is broadly considered a religious practice based on the presence of a particular type of ritual specialist—the *shaman*, or master of the spirits. *Shamanism* is limited to Siberia and other circumpolar areas (e.g., Russian Far North, Scandinavia, and North America). Today, however, the term *shamanism* has been extended to many cultures possessing similar beliefs and practices, such that anthropologists write about *shamans* in New Guinea, South America, etc., and *shamanism* as a general form of religion.

About ten thousand years ago, a great change took place among the world's hunting and gathering peoples, as they began to domesticate plants and animals, develop new productive technologies and complex social institutions, and build and live in cities and other permanent settlements. Subsequently, people also developed a new world view in which man moved to the center of the universe, from where he was destined to control and dominate all nature. This revised cosmology began to spread around the world to neighboring and distant societies and ethnic groups. While many remote and nomadic groups who continued to live by hunting, fishing, and gathering were able to retain their traditional world view for a time, eventually the technologically dominant societies began to expand into their territories as well, bringing with them new cultural values, codes of behavior, beliefs, and teachings.

Nevertheless, many of the ancient stories of egalitarian societies continued to be transmitted from one generation to the next through oral narratives. Certainly, the oral folktales that were told in many different ways thousands of years ago preceded later written versions of these narratives. The process of recording oral tales is extremely important, as writers aim to preserve them for future generations. In the act of writing them down, the tales inevitably become changed to greater or lesser degrees, depending on the recorder's knowledge, background, and the purposes for the recording.[3]

Since these ancient tales have been with us for thousands of years and have undergone so many different changes in the oral tradition, it is often difficult to determine the narrator's ideological intention. Without analyzing this intention, however, it would be impossible for the recorder to reconstruct the ideological meaning of a tale.[4]

As we see in this edition, in contemporary literary folktales based on and derived from the old cultural traditions and oral narratives but later written down and adapted by a given folklorist for a given audience, humans are often held up as the masters of our planet, the ones who control the world and its destiny. The four folktales in this edition exemplify the effects of adaptation of ancient oral narratives to modern written forms and values. In the first three folktales—"The Seven Fears," "The Little Girl Elga," and "The Greedy Kanchuga"—the spirit of the Siberian tiger plays a prominent role; then, in the final story, "Kile Bamba and Loche-The Strongman," a man becomes the central figure, reflecting later ideological notions.

Today, with dramatic climate change and global warming, along with the rapid increase in the world's population and extensive exploitation of natural resources, some creatures—gorillas, whales, polar bears, and Siberian tigers, among others—

---

3 Editor's note: Jack Zipes, *The Great Fairy Tale Tradition: From Straparola and Basile to the Brothers Grimm.* W.W. Norton & Company: New York & London, 2001, p. 846.
4 Editor's note: Ibid., p. 849.

Red cedar panel *Head Canoe* by Steve Brown. Courtesy of the University of Alaska Southeast.

are endangered, and may become extinct in the near future. Alarmed by undeniable changes in the world's physical and ethnic "landscapes," citizens across the globe are rediscovering the wisdom in a traditional world view of our ancestors that acknowledged humans' integral relationship with our environment and the creatures with whom we share it, recognizing that we are not alone on Planet Earth. Mankind undoubtedly cannot live apart from nature and survive when our fellow creatures are gone. Planet Earth may be likened to a grain of sand on a mile-long sandy beach, or, more accurately, to a stone crowded with survivors—innumerable living species marooned on common spherical ground, flying through the universe together.

In a carved panel titled *Head Canoe*,[5] the Alaskan artist Steve Brown depicts raven, bear, frog, eagle, and killer whale traveling together in a traditional Northwest coast canoe. A singular companion accompanies these mythological figures and clan crests—at the front of the canoe a small creature, a person, clings to the gunwales, looking ahead, as they all travel together in harmony.

Ancient oral narratives communicate more than mere fanciful stories, sagas, myths, legends, or folktales; these narratives communicate the views of past human traditions, weaving a complex ethnohistoric record of our relationship with other living species, spiritual worlds, and majestic landscapes. What will happen once the spirits of Whale, Gorilla, Tiger, Polar Bear, Wolf, Eagle, Frog, and other creatures are gone, and Man alone remains adrift in the great canoe called Earth?

Wallace M. Olson
Emeritus Professor of Anthropology
University of Alaska Southeast

---

5   Northwest coast traditional Tlingit and Haida style of canoe, with a raised bow. The panel is displayed at the University of Alaska Southeast William A. Egan Library, Juneau.

INTRODUCTION

The folklore of the aboriginal peoples of the Russian Far East (*see* Figure 1) preserves valuable information for studying the remote past of the Nanays, Nivkhi, Ulchi, Udegeys, Orochi, Negidals, and Oroks. Indeed, their oral narratives survive as both literary and ethnohistoric sources. While oral narratives of people with no written language may or may not yield precise data on historical events, these narratives inevitably offer immense insight into the ancient notions, customs, beliefs, teachings, and economies that framed the productive and spiritual life of the people during various stages of their history.

Figure 1. The Russian Far East Administrative Regions.

The folktale "The Seven Fears" highlights nomadic intolerance for people with a "hare's heart." Among the world's hunting and gathering peoples, there was (and is) nothing more shameful for a hunter than to be known as a coward. In the story, the protagonist, Indiga, sets out on a journey in search of his brother, who has been kidnapped by a tiger. During the search, Indiga experiences seven fears and survives seven tests of bravery to earn back his courage and his human heart. Indiga is able to restore his self-confidence and earn the trust of his peers only by facing the Siberian tiger.

"The Little Girl Elga" is historically tied to the ancient concept of womankind as creator of people and animals. In this folktale, Elga, a rebellious daughter and courageous hunter, disobeys her parents' wishes and acts against the conventional role of women in society, killing a tiger to protect villagers from its aggressive attacks. Furthermore, Elga overcomes her evil stepmother's malice by defeating her with a magical implement.

In an egalitarian society, greed is condemned and sharing is admired, especially during times of economic hardship, epidemic, or natural disaster. "The Greedy Kanchuga" teaches a lesson to individuals who place their own well-being and interests above the common good. In the folktale, the protagonist tiger-man rises victorious over antagonist Kanchuga's evil intentions and greed for food.

The folktale "Kile Bamba and Loche-The Strongman" should be understood in its historic context. Beginning in the seventeenth century, during Russia's expansion into the Far East, Russian settlers came in close contact with the aboriginal people of Siberia and non-Russian merchants engaged in various commercial undertakings with the indigenous population of Siberia and the Far East. Subsequently, the Russian *promyshlenniki*[6] and *Cossacks*[7] collided with Chinese merchants over the far eastern territory and its resources. Because Chinese merchants had operated in the area prior to the arrival of the Russians, a Russian-Chinese territorial dispute arose over control of the land and people of the Amur River estuary.

The *Nerchinsk Treaty*, signed in 1689 between Russian and Chinese officialdoms, specified the rules and boundaries for the region under dispute. However, despite the *Treaty*, frequent conflicts, tensions, and violations of the agreement persisted, entangling the indigenous people of the region in the Russian-Chinese rivalry for control of the Amur territory.

The folktale "Kile Bamba and Loche-The Strongman" was written down, published, and censored during the Soviet period of Russian history. It therefore favors the friendly Russian character Ivan, a good neighbor, over the "devilish" Chinese merchant Li-Chan, who takes advantage of the Native people's trust and *naiveté* and drives them to economic ruin. Ivan is portrayed in the folktale as a true friend, liberator, and fair

---

6 Commercial people, traders.

7 Free Russian peasants commonly recruited by the tsar's government to serve in the army. Russian *Cossacks* also were among the first explorers of Siberia, the Russian Far East, and North America in the seventeenth and eighteenth centuries. Over the years, aboriginal people of the Russian Far North and North America have thus come to use this word to describe a white man.

partner of aboriginal people. In other words, the emotion that Nagishkin seeks to evoke is somewhat ideologically skewed, politicized, and censored by the former Soviet authorities, thus detracting from the tale's traditional sense of the miraculous.

Folktales of the Russian Far East served three main purposes: to explain, to teach, and to exemplify how to behave in society. Such folktales, then, could be said to have provided a moral directive, if not an authoritative ethical code. They also examined the extent to which a man is a victim of circumstances and the extent to which he brings his destiny upon himself.

Alexander B. Dolitsky
Alaska-Siberia Research Center

ETHNOGRAPHIC INFORMATION

According to the 2002 census,[8] there live in Russia's southern Far East (i.e., the Amur River drainage basin) 12,000 Nanays; 5,000 Nivkhi; 3,000 Ulchi; 2,000 Udegeys; 1,000 Orochi; 1,000 Negidals; and 400 Oroks (*see* Figures 2, 3).

Nanays, Oroks, Orochi, Udegeys, and Ulchi speak languages that belong to the Manchu division of the Tunguso-Manchu branch of the Uralo-Altaic language family. The Manchu are divided into two closely related language groups: Nani and Udegey. The Nani group comprises the Nanay, Ulchi, Orok, and Orochi languages. These peoples are closely related ethnically, culturally, and linguistically; they all speak closely related dialects of the Nani language group. The Udegey forms an independent group in the Manchu division of the Uralo-Altaic language family. The Negidal language belongs to the Tungusic division. Negidal is basically Evenk with many Orochi and

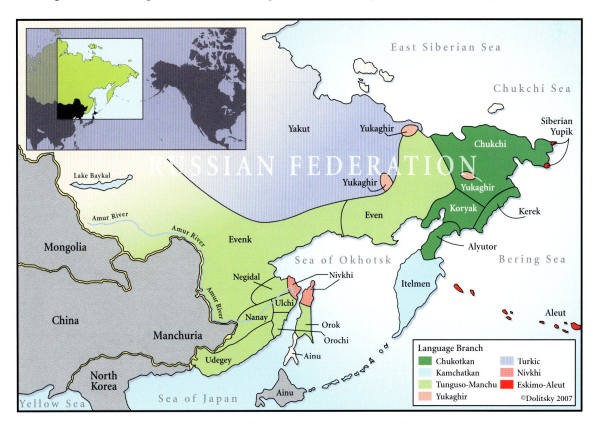

Figure 2. Populations and Speakers of the Asian North Pacific Region Languages.

---

8 Национальная Принадлежность и Владение Русским Языком. [National Identity and Knowledge of the Russian Language]. *Всероссийская перепись населения 2002 года. Федеральная служба государственной статистики,* 2004 www.gks.ru/perepis/t5.htm.

Udegey linguistic elements. The Nivkhi are a *Paleoasiatic*[9] people whose culture is closely related to the four Manchu peoples (Nanays, Oroks, Orochi, and Ulchi) among whom they live; there has been much borrowing of cultural traditions and language elements between the Nivkhi and Manchu peoples.[10]

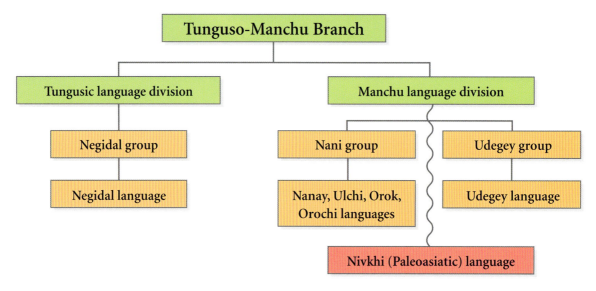

Figure 3. Uralo-Altaic Language Family.

The indigenous population of the Amur River drainage basin in the Russian Far East (i.e., the Amur-Ussuri region of Primorye and Khabarovsk *Krays*[11]) was of an all-embracing character; their subsistence activities were primarily based on *taiga*[12] hunting, sea fur-animal trading, fishing, and gathering. Large animal hunting was pursued year-round as needed, while the hunting of animals for fur was pursued for three or four months in the winter. All hunting grounds were distributed among clans and families and frequently were located quite remotely from their abodes. Various wild animals served not only as food, but also as principal material for the manufacture of clothing. This clothing varied according to its purpose and the time of year in which it was worn.

---

9 Under the term *Paleoasiatic,* ethnographers group, on the basis of languages, several Siberian and Far East peoples, among whom are the Yukaghirs, Koryaks, Chukchi, Asiatic Eskimos, Kereks, Itelmen, Nivkhi, and Ainu.

10 Ronald Wixman, *The Peoples of the USSR: An Ethnographic Handbook.* M.E. Sharpe, Inc. Armonk, N.Y., 1988, pp. 130, 145.

11 *Kray* is a large administrative and territorial unit, which supersedes *oblast* and *rayon* districts. The literal meaning of *kray* in the Slavic languages is "edge," reflecting the original pioneering nature of the *kray*. There were nine *krays* in the territory of the former Soviet Union: six in Russia and three in Kazakhstan.

12 The Russian word *taiga* refers to the dense, marshy forest lands of the northern hemisphere.

As to their religious adherence, the indigenous peoples in the lower basin of the Amur River were *animists*; they believed that the world was populated with spirits. Common spirits were called *sven* and evil spirits were called *amban*. The intermediaries between the people and the spirits were the *shamans*[13] or "medicine men." Today, the religions of the indigenous peoples of the Russian Far East comprise, basically, a mixture of *animist-shaminist*, Eastern Orthodox, and Chinese beliefs.

Alexander B. Dolitsky
Alaska-Siberia Research Center

---

[13] *Shaman*, a Russian word from the Tungus language, is an anthropologist's name for a village spiritual leader or healer. According to the religious ideas of many northern peoples, the *shaman* was a person chosen by spirits and other supernatural creatures to fill the role of an intermediary between people and the other worlds.

ABOUT THE SIBERIAN TIGER

The Siberian tiger (*Panthera tigris altaica*) is a rare subspecies of tiger (*P. tigris*). Also known as the Amur, North Chinese, Manchurian, or Korean tiger, it is presently native to the Amur River drainage basin in the Russian Far East (i.e., the Amur-Ussuri region of Primorye and Khabarovsk *Krays*), where it inhabits forests in shrub-covered mountainsides up to an elevation of three thousand feet (*see* Figure 4). Although tigers live in forests, they are not particularly good tree climbers.

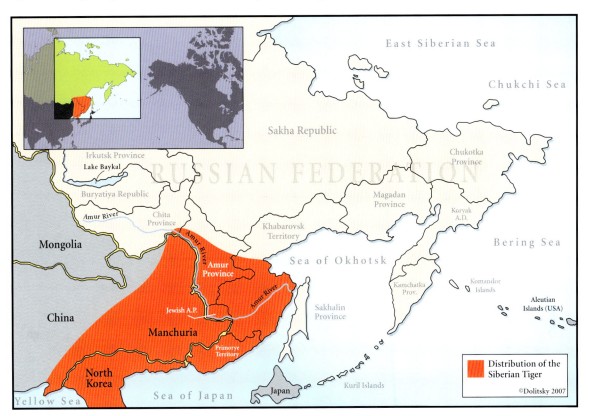

Figure 4. Historic Distribution of the Siberian Tiger.

The Siberian tiger is the largest member of the cat family, with a lifespan of up to twenty-five years. Mature males normally reach a head and body length of 190–220 centimeters (6.2–7.2 ft) and a height of about 107 cm (3.5 ft) at shoulder. One particularly large male has been documented as measuring 350 cm (11.5 ft) from the nose to the tip of the tail in total length. Although male Siberian tigers commonly weigh up to 280 kilograms (617 lb), the average male weighs around 230 kg (507 lb). Weights of up to 306 kg (674 lb) have been recorded. Females, smaller than males, generally weigh between 100–168 kg (220–370 lb), but can weigh as much as 180 kg (396 lb).

Siberian tiger. Oil on canvas by Jason Morgan.

Apart from its size, the Siberian tiger is differentiated from other tiger subspecies by paler fur and dark brown stripes. Some have white patches with black markings around the muzzle, eyes, ears, and on the chest. No two tigers have the same pattern of stripes; since the face markings are so distinctive, they can be used like fingerprints to tell them apart. A small number of tigers are whitish with dark brown stripes and ice-blue eyes, but these are rare. The fur of the Siberian tiger is thicker and longer than that of other tigers, presumably in order to cope with the freezing temperatures of the tiger's habitat. Siberian tigers differ, too, in that their feet are larger than those of most other tiger subspecies; this facilitates passage through snow.

Siberian tigers move with an elegance that conceals their tremendous strength. Through powerful vocal chords, their cries range from barks, coughs, and hisses to great roars. Hearing is acute in Siberian tigers; smell and sight are less well developed. Although Siberian tigers are normally nocturnal, with night vision more than five times better than humans', they may be active in daylight during the winter months.

The Siberian tiger is a solitary animal, except during courting and when the female has cubs. Gestation lasts approximately three and one-half months. Typically, two to four cubs are born—blind and helpless, each weighing about two pounds. The female rears her young alone. Cubs depend on their mother for food for approximately eighteen months.

Tigers hunt on the ground, mainly at night; they generally hunt alone. Their canine teeth are their most important weapon; their silent, padded paws, which feature retractile claws, are also equally deadly. Even though tigers prefer to pounce on smaller prey, they will hunt larger animals by stalking and attacking them in a silent rush. After the kill, they will eat what they need and hide the remains, returning to the carcass until it is consumed. A tiger does not always catch its prey, and it may be successful in only one out of ten to twenty tries.

Like all other cats, the Siberian tiger is a carnivorous predator; an adept hunter, it preys primarily on wild boar and red deer. Both species make up 65–90 percent of the tigers' diet in the Russian Far East. Other important prey species include moose, elk, roe deer, Sitka deer, lynx, and musk deer. Even fierce animals like adult brown bears

Siberian tiger. Oil on canvas by Jason Morgan.

rank among the prey of the Siberian tiger. Asiatic black and brown bears constitute 5–8 percent of the Siberian tiger's diet; but the tiger will also take smaller prey like hares, rabbits, and fish. Tigers occasionally kill wolves to reduce competition over their limited prey base. Thus, where there are more tigers, wolves cease to exist.

The Siberian tiger is critically endangered. In the early 1900s, it lived throughout northeastern China, the Korean Peninsula, northeastern Mongolia, and southeastern Russia. Today, it is largely confined to a very small part of Russia's southern Far East. By the 1940s, the estimated population was down to fewer than fifty in the Russian Far East, although some hundreds still populate neighboring China.

A count taken in 1996 reported 430 Siberian tigers in the wild. Russian conservation efforts have led to a slight increase, or at least to a stabilized population of the subspecies. The number of individuals in the forests of Russia's southern Far East was estimated to be between 431 and 529 in the most recent count, in 2005.[14]

Alexander B. Dolitsky
Alaska-Siberia Research Center

---

14 http://news.nationalgeographic.com/news/2005/06/0616_050616_siberiantiger.html

THE TYGER

by William Blake
1757–1827

TYGER, Tyger, burning bright
In the forests of the night:
What immortal hand or eye
Could frame thy fearful symmetry?

In what distant deeps or skies
Burnt the fire of thine eyes?
On what wings dare he aspire?
What the hand dare seize the fire?

And what shoulder, & what art
Could twist the sinews of thy heart?
And when thy heart began to beat,
What dread hand? & what dread feet?

What the hammer? what the chain?
In what furnace was thy brain?
What the anvil? what dread grasp
Dare its deadly terrors clasp?

When the stars threw down their spears,
And watered heaven with their tears:
Did He smile His work to see?
Did He who made the lamb make thee?

Tyger, Tyger, burning bright
In the forests of the night:
What immortal hand or eye
Dare frame thy fearful symmetry?

Siberian tiger. Oil on canvas
by Jason Morgan.

15 Gordon J.L. Ramel's poem is a parody of the earlier poem *The Tyger*, written by William Blake (1757–1827) in 1794. Blake's original poem is refined in its rhythm and prose, but emphasized only the tiger's ferociousness. Gordon J.L. Ramel conveys a timely message by focusing on the spiritual crisis of the human species that has extirpated the tiger from much of its former range and made it an endangered species—no matter how ferocious the tiger, the human species is far more dangerous. The poem was originally copyrighted by Ramel using the spelling *Tyger Tyger Revisited*.

TIGER TIGER REVISITED[15]

by Gordon J.L. Ramel

TIGER, tiger, fading fast
in the shadow we have cast.
What brave law or business deal
can thy future's safety seal?

What the future, what the hope
that human kind may learn to cope
with life and maintenance of breath
without this need of needless death?

In what sulfurous cauldron groans
the mind that lives to sell your bones;
and in what moral poverty
live those who take thy life from thee?

What the learning, what the thought
values a life like yours as naught,
in what science or machine
can beauty such as yours be seen?

Who did he hate who sowed the seed
of human ignorance and greed;
and can he smile our work to see
as we who killed the Lamb kill thee?

TIGER, tiger, fading fast
from the present to the past.
How can mere humanity
so quickly still thy majesty?

Siberian tiger. Oil on canvas by Jason Morgan.

THE SEVEN FEARS

It was still the time when a Udegey, looking at a stone, saw a stone-man; looking at a bear, he thought he saw a bear-man; looking at a fish, he thought he saw a water-man; looking at a tree, he thought he saw a tree-man. In those times all sorts of things happened to people. Such things happened that nowadays do not.

There were two brothers—Solomdiga and Indiga. They lived in the upper reaches of the Koppi River.

The father had died. But before he died he told them:

"Always stay with one another. If something bad happens to one, let the other help him. Both of you look in the same direction. Do what I just told you."

When their father died, the brothers entwined[16] a white plait into his braided hair. They placed him in a grave with his feet pointing east so that even after death he could see the sun rise. For seven days they brought food to their father; they fed his spirit.

Then they went hunting.

"Both of you look in the same direction," the father had told the brothers. But the younger brother Indiga walked behind his brother and looked in all directions. Indiga was very fast with his eyes; he did not like to look in one direction.

---

16 To twine around or together.

The brothers walked and walked. Indiga looked to all sides. Suddenly he heard a noise. He looked around and saw a tiger bounding at his brother from the bushes! His brother could not use his spear or draw his knife in time. Indiga was farther away. He should have thrown his spear at the tiger! But Indiga became frightened like a hare. He threw himself to the ground, folded his arms, and begged the tiger to go away—to leave him and his brother alone.

Indiga lay there for a long time. When he finally lifted his head to look, the tiger and his brother, Solomdiga, were not there. Both had disappeared. Indiga's heart started aching. He called his brother. He called and called, but nobody answered. Only the mountains echoed his calls:

"So-so-lo-lom! Di-di! Ga-ga! A-a-a!"

Indiga began to cry. How could he live without his brother? What would he say to his kin? How would he throw the shame off his face?

Indiga cried and cried, but there was nothing he could do—at home his mother was waiting. He needed to continue hunting.

So Indiga started looking for traps. In one of them was a weasel. As soon as the weasel saw Indiga, he called out to him:

"Go away, you brother-loser!" He chewed off his own leg, which had been caught in the trap, and scampered off.

Next Indiga looked at the snares. A polecat was sitting in one of the nooses. When the polecat saw Indiga, he began to yell at him:

"How can I possibly give myself to you? You're disgusting—you've lost your brother!" The polecat tore the noose to pieces and walked off into the *taiga*.[17]

Then Indiga shot a goose. The arrow hit the goose below its wing. The goose tore out the arrow with its beak, threw it back at Indiga, and yelled at the lad:

"Why should I fall prey to such a person? Indiga lost his brother!" So saying, the goose flew to the middle of the river, folded his wings, hurled himself into the water, and drowned.

After that, neither animals nor birds would give themselves as prey to the one with a frightened hare's heart.

Indiga sat down and began to think. He thought for a long time. He smoked all of his tobacco; he smoked all of the dry moss around him. His heart was aching. Indiga thought: "So, I've lost my brother. It's a bad thing to lose a brother. My heart aches. You lose a pipe, and you're not satisfied until you find it! I lost Solomdiga, my brother . . . And I'm going to search for him. If I find him, my heart will stop aching! If I die, my heart will stop aching!"

Indiga went to his mother and sank to his knees. He told her all. He told her how his heart became like that of a hare. His mother kissed Indiga. In tears, she said to him:

"Your father taught both of you to look ahead. You did not listen to him. Now you've lost your brother, and you've found in yourself a hare's heart. Go and search for a man's heart. Go seek your brother. He disappeared because of your fright. You'll bring him back only by being brave!"

Indiga took his pipe, a steel fire-striker, his knife, and a spear, and set out. Unsure which way to go, he headed in the direction of the setting sun . . .

He met a creeping snake and asked him where he should go to find his brother. The snake did not know. He went on farther. He met with a mouse running on the ground and asked her if she had seen Solomdiga. The mouse had not seen him. Indiga went on

---

17 Boreal forest.

farther. He saw a squirrel climbing in the trees and asked her. No, the squirrel had not seen his brother. He came to a river and saw fish swimming in it. He asked the fish if they had seen Solomdiga. The fish had not seen him either. Indiga went on. He asked a jumping frog. The frog had not seen him. He saw a flying wren and asked her. The wren answered that she had not seen Solomdiga—she flies low. He asked a crane that flies higher. The crane had not seen him either, but suggested:

"Ask the eagle, he flies higher than anybody."

Indiga began to ask the eagle if he had seen where the tiger took his brother Solomdiga.

The eagle answered to him:

"Your brother is far away! He can be found if you endure seven fears. Now you have the heart of a frightened hare. When your heart becomes like that of a brave man, you'll find your brother!"

The eagle then plucked out one of his feathers and said:

"I'll help you. Wherever my feather flies—you follow it!"

As the feather flew toward the sunset, Indiga followed.

How long he walked, who knows? He crossed three brooks. The feather flew ahead of him. Indiga looked directly ahead, as his father had taught him, and strode on, having lost his brother.

Finally, he came to a river. The eagle's feather flew over the river. Indiga made a boat and floated it in the water. The water boiled as if it were in a kettle… Steam arose out of it. Fog formed in the lowland. Indiga's boat began to shrivel and warp, and sink. The fish that had boiled floated to the surface belly-up and looked at Indiga with their white eyes. The scene struck terror in him. But Indiga knew work had to be done, or his heart would remain that of a frightened hare forever. Indiga said to himself: "This is not fright yet. Fright is still ahead of me."

Indiga placed his bow between two trees overhanging the river, their trunks anchored on the banks. He pulled back the bowstring and secured it with a twig. He placed an arrow on the bowstring. With one hand he grasped the arrow, and with the other he broke the twig. The twig rebounded. The bowstring broke loose. The bow unbent. The arrow flew. It carried Indiga over the boiling river. The steam swirled up, scorching him. Indiga suffered . . . The river was wide. As he flew, the lad became scorched all over. "It's nothing," he thought. "It'll heal."

The arrow dropped on the other bank. Indiga got to his feet. He saw the eagle's feather waiting for him. As soon as the lad reached ground the feather flew farther. Indiga walked after it.

He walked and walked . . . He jumped over three brooks, he climbed over three hills. Between two mountains he saw a stony clearing. A narrow path led to the clearing. The path was dotted with bones and fenced in by skulls. Indiga was frightened. And the eagle's feather flew down that little path directly to the clearing. Indiga saw that in the clearing there was a den of the tigers. There were as many tigers as there are bees in a beehive! They were tearing their prey to pieces. They were caressing each other. They were lunging at each other. The tigers were roaring so that it sounded like a thunderstorm over the den.

The eagle's feather flew through the den.

Indiga stopped. His heart was pounding. "They're going to eat me!" he thought.

"Let me smoke a pipe, perhaps for the last time," Indiga said to himself. As he finished smoking, he suddenly remembered the fire-striker. From the tinder-fungus around him, he pulled out dry grass and plaited it. He put the plaited grass on his head. He struck a fire and set it to the plait.

The dry grass atop Indiga's head blazed like a bonfire. Indiga rushed through the den of the tigers. The tigers dashed aside in every direction. They saw nothing except the fire; they did not see Indiga! The tigers roared, they beat the ground with their tails; their red mouths gaped. And Indiga passed by them. He said to himself: "It's obvious that this is not fright. Fright is still to come to me." He ran through the den. He killed a tiger and drank its blood. He took its meat with him and also its hide.

The eagle's feather, once again above Indiga, flew on. It did not fly over a path; it flew in a straight line. Indiga jumped over three brooks, climbed over three hills, and passed over three rivers. After the last river, the forest began.

In the forest, the trees reached to the heavens and grew thick. Sunlight cannot penetrate such branches, nor can the wind blow. Such trees are covered with the entwined roots of plants, and the boughs twist and snatch at you as if they were hands. The boughs let animals through, but not a man. Indiga saw that somebody's bones on the branches had already started to whiten; and he became very frightened. His heart pounding and his hands trembling, he said to himself: "Obviously this is not fright yet. Fright is yet to come." He put on the tiger's hide, cut the meat in pieces, and strung the pieces on his spear. Indiga went into the forest.

The trees stretched toward Indiga, for they sensed the smell of the meat. With their hands-branches they groped for Indiga. When a branch inclined toward him, Indiga threw a piece of meat, and the trees wrested the meat from each other. The trees began to fight for the meat. They lashed each other with their twigs so hard that their bark and even wood chips flew in all directions. Indiga went farther and farther into the forest, following the eagle's feather. He took with him some branches of the trees, thinking, "I'll light a fire when it becomes possible to do so."

The eagle's feather flew on. Indiga jumped six brooks, climbed over six hills, and crossed six rivers.

Soon he came to a marsh. The feather flew over it in a straight line. What was Indiga to do? He started throwing the branches onto the marsh to make places to step. But the branches sank into the marsh's water, and the marsh started to bubble. Small blue lights began to flutter over it. Treading carefully, Indiga came to the middle of the marsh. In his way stood a small hunchbacked man who had only one leg and one arm. Indiga became frightened. His heart was pounding; his hands and feet were shaking. Although he had never seen the man, Indiga recognized him. The man was called Boko. He does only bad things to people. He leads people into the marsh so that the quagmire can suck them in.

Boko asked:

"Where are you going, my lad?"

"I'm looking for you," replied Indiga. (What could he lose? He had nothing to lose!)

"Here I am," Boko said. "Why do you need me for?"

"I've heard from people," said Indiga, "that your one leg is stronger than two. I can't believe that. That's why I came here. Let's see who can jump higher. Where I come from nobody can jump higher than I can."

"Go ahead, jump," said Boko.

Indiga jumped. He jumped higher than the trees. He came down with his legs widespread and landed on the branches. He sank into the marsh up to his waist. The branches saved him from drowning.

Boko laughed.

"Really! Is that how they jump?" he laughed. "Here's how it should be!"

He squatted on his one leg, then straightened it out—and how he jumped! He soared to the clouds, turned his head to look below, and came hurtling back.

Meanwhile, Indiga continued to throw branches to get out of the marsh . . .

When Boko landed, he sank deep into the quagmire. While he was getting out of it and wiping his eyes, Indiga reached firm ground. He stood on a level place. Now he had no fear of Boko.

Indiga said to himself: "That still was not fright. Really, fright must be ahead of me."

Boko cried out to him:

"Hey boy, did you see how you have to jump? Come here!"

"There's no time!" cried Indiga. "I have other things to do."

And the eagle's feather flew farther. Indiga could not dry himself. Covered with mud, he went farther. He jumped over nine brooks and climbed over nine hills. When his high fur boots were worn through, Indiga went on barefooted. With aching feet, he walked around nine lakes.

Out from the last of the lakes a large snake crawled. His stony scales glittered; his scales were ringing. Flames shot out of his mouth. Under the snake, the grass was on fire. The snake breathed on Indiga—his clothes caught fire, his eyebrows were singed. Indiga felt awful. He grew pale. His heart pounded, his hands and feet shook, and his forehead dripped with sweat. The lad consoled himself: "Really, this is not fright yet. Fright is still ahead." He mustered his courage and cried out to the snake:

"Hey, if you want to eat me, take first a piece of fat bacon! Will one piece be enough for you?"

He picked up a stone, scraped the quagmire mud from his body, smeared the mud on the stone, and tossed it into the snake's mouth.

The snake choked. It could not swallow the stone. And it could not breathe fire on Indiga. Indiga ran away.

And the eagle's feather flew straight ahead, not following a path.

Indiga jumped over nine brooks, climbed over nine hills, walked around nine lakes, and passed through nine forests. He walked barefooted, bloodying his soles on the stones. Eventually, he entered a stony ravine.

Then something frightening happened—around him the stones came to life! Turning around, they followed him with their eyes, swaying to and fro, talking to each other in stone language. And the feather flew farther; Indiga went after it.

Suddenly Indiga spotted a man standing among the stones. Not an ordinary man. His head was radish-shaped, his legs bent, and his stature such that one had to look upward in order to see his face. Indiga had not met anything like this before, but he knew at once who was standing before him. It was Kakzamu, the vicious mountain-man. Indiga became white in the face; his heart began to pound; his hands and feet shook; his hair stood on end from the fright. But he told himself: "This is not fright yet. Fright is to come." He bowed to Kakzamu.

Kakzamu asked:

"What do you want here?"

Indiga told him (figuring himself already dead):

"Hey, neighbor, they say that you are very strong!"

"They speak the truth," Kakzamu replied. "Do you see all the boulders around you? All of them were once people, but I've turned them to stone. I must guard my cliff and everything that's below it. Now I'm going to turn you into stone!"

He touched Indiga's arm. Indiga's arm turned to stone. Indiga could not shake his arm; he could not lift it. His arm turned black. Indiga almost died of fright.

But he regained his courage and said:

"Eh, eh, my grandfather knew how to do this long ago! It doesn't take great strength to turn a living thing into stone! Can you turn stone into living flesh? My grandfather knew how to do it, but he died long ago."

Kakzamu said to Indiga:

"My strength is in my power. Whatever I want to do, I'll do!"

He touched Indiga's arm. The arm came back to life. Hot blood ran into it and the arm began to shake.

"Eh, eh, that's not all yet!" Indiga cried out. "Now bend over to me, and I'll whisper into your ear what my grandfather knew, but took with him when he died!"

The mountain-man bent toward Indiga. He offered his ear. He was rolling his eyes. His nostrils were so big that a clenched fist could be put in one of them. Indiga took from his belt a tobacco pouch and emptied all of the tobacco into Kakzamu's nostril.

Kakzamu began to sneeze. He sneezed and sneezed . . . All his strength went into his nose. Before he regained his strength, time had gone by . . . And Indiga had run, run far away from Kakzamu.

Indiga followed the eagle's feather again. He jumped over a brook, climbed over three mountains, walked around six lakes, and passed through nine forests. He walked his feet to the bone.

Indiga walked and walked until he came upon a wall of stone. He tried to go around the wall, but couldn't find an opening. He tried to climb it, but fell. To the left, to the right—the wall stretched across the land; its top was hidden in the clouds.

The eagle's feather hit the wall and turned into dust, as if it had never existed.

Indiga began to feel awful. So awful that there aren't words to describe it. That wall—so tough you couldn't break through it by strength! That wall—so smart you couldn't overcome it by cunning! Indiga began to cry when he looked at himself. His feet were worn to the bone. His arms were scorched. His clothing was in shreds. And he was hungry—his stomach stuck to his spine. Indiga had endured many trials, and still he had not met his brother! Indiga took out his knife and cried out:

"I'm not going back, none of my relatives have ever gone back. I'm going to cut out my hare's heart . . . I'm going to wipe off the shame from my face . . ."

He put the knife to his chest, and was about to end it all, when suddenly he noticed a door in the wall. "What terrors lie beyond this?" wondered Indiga.

Indiga composed himself: "What do I have to fear? I am a man!"

Suddenly he heard a man's heart beating in his chest. He took a spear in his hand. He hit the door with all his might. The door opened wide. Ready for anything, Indiga passed through the door, crouching low . . .

But what's this?

Indiga saw he was at the very place where he had lost his brother. And the wall simply disappeared.

All around Indiga white lilies burned fire red, the birds were chirping . . .

And directly in front of him stood his brother Solomdiga. His brother stood there holding the hand of a beautiful girl. Indiga had never seen such a beautiful girl. She had eyebrows like thin rushes; her eyes were yellow, shining like the sun. The girl was dressed in a yellow wedding gown. The gown was marked with black bands, such as tigers have.

Solomdiga said to Indiga:

"Thank you brother! You were afraid of nothing for my sake!"

The girl smiled at Indiga. She said:

"I'm a woman of the tiger family. I fell in love with your brother. That's why I carried him away. But when I saw that you couldn't live without your brother, I got permission from the Master Tiger to become a simple person. Now I'll be living with you. It will be easy to live with you; you are brave people!"

They all held hands and walked together.

The lads' mother was happy.

Solomdiga and the tiger-girl became man and wife.

And Indiga learned to look forward. Never again did he have a hare's heart.

The end.

Connect to Your Life

Are courage and bravery important values in your culture? Have you ever been faced with a difficult situation where you felt like you "chickened out"? Did other people seem braver than you? With a partner, discuss a situation like that from your own life. What lessons might be learned from your experience?

THE LITTLE GIRL ELGA

This happened very long ago, even before the old Udegey's time. Udegey's grandfather told him about this. And his grandfather's father had told him. It was very long ago.

A wife of the hunter Soldiga died, leaving him a little daughter, Elga.

Soldiga buried his wife, grieved a little, and married a second time. The woman he wed was named Puninga. The threesome lived together: Soldiga, his wife Puninga, and daughter, Elga.

Soldiga loved his daughter very much. He made many toys for her: a rocking cradle, little houses, and a brake tool for kneading hides. He made these toys to get Elga used to woman's work.

But little Elga begged of her father:

"Make a sled, bow, arrows, and a spear for me!"

Hearing this, Puninga asked:

"Why do you need the toys of a boy?"

"When I grow up I'll help my father in hunting," answered Elga.

"What next!" Puninga exclaimed. "That's not your work."

Soldiga looked at his daughter and realized that a brave little girl was growing up in his family. He made the toys for his daughter: a small sled, a cross-bow, and a

spear. He also carved a tiny wooden reindeer and tiny sled dogs, and gear for riding reindeer.

Seeing that her husband did not listen to her, Puninga took a dislike to Elga. She started to treat her badly whenever her father was off hunting. Elga suffered through this, and never complained about her stepmother; she didn't want to distress her father.

So they lived on.

Then one day Soldiga saw a wild boar in the *taiga*. Soldiga chased after him for a long time. Exhausted, the boar crawled into a thicket and lay down.

The tiger-*amban*[18] passed by. He was hungry. He came upon the boar—and how he tore at him! Unable to see what the commotion was about, Soldiga threw his spear into the thicket. The spear went through the boar and brushed against the tiger-*amban*.

---

18 The indigenous peoples of the Amur area were *animists*; they believed that the world was populated with spirits: common ones called *sven* and evil ones called *amban*.

The tiger-*amban* became furious and hurled himself at Soldiga. The hunter began to say to the tiger that he did not want to kill him, that he was aiming at the boar; but the tiger did not listen to Soldiga and tore him to pieces.

Thus the tiger got to know the taste of human flesh and blood. He began to come to the camp. Other hunters in the camp followed Soldiga's path—begging the tiger to leave them alone, begging him to go to other places for food. But the tiger did not listen to them. He started to come by night, dragging away pigs, reindeer, and small dogs. He started dragging away small children. What could be worse?

Meanwhile, without her father, life got very bad for Elga. Puninga came to hate her. She exhausted the girl with work. Elga had to get the water, wash the cereal for the porridge, salt the fish, dry the fish for the small dogs, drag brushwood from the *taiga* forest for the fire . . . Puninga would lie for days on the sleeping bench—resting, eating, sleeping, smoking a pipe, and doing nothing herself—all the while yelling at Elga: "Give me this, give me that!"

Elga knew that she had to listen to the older people, and she did everything her stepmother commanded her to do. It was very difficult for Elga. But she suffered on. She comforted herself with the following thoughts: "When I grow up, I'm going to leave my stepmother. I'm going to live by myself. I'm going to hunt."

Elga never parted with her spear, because her father had made it. And Elga loved her father very much. Wherever she went, she took the spear with her.

Then one day her stepmother sent Elga to strip birch bark for the making of a new basket.

The girl went to the *taiga*, found a good birch, made two incisions, and began to strip the bark. Suddenly she heard somebody asking her in a gruff voice:

"Hey, what are you doing here, little girl? Who are you?"

Elga turned around and saw a tiger-*amban*. For a long time hunting had been bad for him. His sides sunken from hunger, the tiger appeared very vicious. But Elga was not frightened by the tiger. She answered him:

"I'm Soldiga's daughter. And what do you want?"

The tiger replied:

"I've torn Soldiga to pieces . . . and now I'm going to eat you!"

Elga yelled at the tiger:

"Go away, thief!"

The tiger hurled himself at Elga. But the girl jumped to the other side of the birch. The birch bent down and shielded her. With all his strength the tiger hit the birch with his head, smashing against it.

Elga pointed her spear at him:

"Go away thief, or it's going to be bad for you!"

The tiger began to roar so loudly that the leaves of the birches fell to the forest floor. He jumped again. Now two of the birches bent down and held him. The tiger was stuck; in no way could he get out. As much as he tried, he could not free himself from the trap. The birches held him tight. Elga threw her spear at him. The spear entered one of his eye sockets and came out of the other. Blinded by Elga's spear, the tiger died.

Elga skinned the striped hide off the tiger and returned to the camp.

She saw that people were putting belongings in baskets, taking down their *yurtas*.[19] They were gathering together to go away, they were so afraid of the tiger. Elga called out to them:

"Where are you going? The tiger won't come here any more!"

"What do you know, little girl!" said the oldest Udegey. "The tiger has come here, and he'll come here again. We're leaving because we want to escape death!"

Elga showed the tiger's hide to the elders:

"I'm telling you that the tiger-*amban* will not come here again! Here, I've skinned the tiger's hide."

The Udegeys became frightened.

"What have you done, girl?" they cried. "A tiger should not be killed. Now his spirit will come to the camp in the night and destroy us all! The *taiga* will reach to our camp; grass will grow on our paths; marsh will cover this place . . ."

Elga replied:

"I know the rules of the hunters. I twice asked the tiger to leave. But he did not listen."

"Well, now that's different," said the elders. "The tiger himself is to blame!"

The Udegeys did not leave. They began to praise the girl.

It was distressing to Puninga that they did not praise her. She was altogether embittered with her stepdaughter. Whatever the girl did, she could not please Puninga. Elga washed the cereal, cooked the porridge; then Puninga came by and threw the cereal out, or said it had to be washed again.

One day Elga was sewing a dress. Puninga said she wasn't doing it right.

"What are you doing? You, with crooked hands!" she said. "Don't you know how to sew? Take it apart and do it over again. But do it better, with brighter colors and a better design."

---

19 The y*urta* is a tent used by Siberian nomads as a shelter. Made of felt stretched over a light wood framework and able to be disassembled in less than an hour, it has been called the best portable dwelling developed by man. The *yurta* is cylindrical with a dome top. A wattle wall about five feet high is topped with a wooden frame for the dome. Inside, carpets cover the bare earth.

Puninga yelled at her and cursed her. Elga, beginning to cry, carried the dress out of the *yurta*-tent and went to the bank of the river, where she sat down among the ferns. She sat there and cried. The ferns began to stir, murmuring.

One of the ferns asked Elga:

"Why are you crying, little girl?"

Elga told the fern how difficult her life was. The fern patted her with its shaggy leaves and said:

"Don't cry, little girl! This bitterness can be easily helped. We'll help you."

The fern then began to invite all the flowers and grasses to help Elga. All sorts of flowers and grasses stretched themselves over the dress. They lay down on it and with various curls they twisted themselves into it. What a beautiful pattern they formed on the dress! Elga had never seen anything like that before.

Then the fern collected all of Elga's tears, sprinkled them on the dress, and the pattern remained fixed on it.

The fern said to Elga:

"I'm so sorry for you, Elga! When your stepmother hurts you, you cry so much that your tears soak this soil; we have grown on your tears. So we've helped you the only way we could."

Elga carried the dress back to the camp. In the camp there lived many women who did fine needlework. When they saw the pattern on Elga's dress, they opened their mouths wide in envy and astonishment. They had never seen a dress like that!

Puninga became even more embittered with Elga.

"I want a dress made of reindeer hide!" she said to Elga.

But it was summer. At that time, the hair of a reindeer is short. Where could Elga get a hide with long hair?

Elga walked through the camp asking the neighbors, but nobody could help her.

So she sat down and began to cry again. She started to finger her toys. Remembering her father with tender thoughts, even more tears gushed from her eyes.

Suddenly the toy reindeer Elga's father had made said to the girl:

"Don't cry, little mistress, your misery can be helped!"

The reindeer shook himself. With his little feet he stamped the floor and began to grow. He grew and grew—and became big. His hide was covered with white winter hair. He shook the hide off himself—and became small again.

Elga made a new dress. Her hands were prickled all over by the sharp hair. And again her stepmother was not pleased.

"You did not make this! Somebody is helping you . . . All of this is to no purpose. You'll never embroider like I do. When I make a dress for myself, you'll see how it is to be done! Run to the camp at the Anyuy River. That's where my grandmother

lives. Ask her for my needle. And see to it that you return in the morning. Don't be late!"

But it is a long way to the camp at the Anyuy River—it takes several days to get there.

What was Elga to do? Again she became sad. She fingered her toys, remembering her father in tender thoughts. Suddenly she heard a voice:

"Don't be sad, my little mistress, what are we here for?"

Elga looked around. In front of her there stood an entire team of little dogs. Twelve little dogs, one more beautiful than the other! They were wagging their fluffy tails. They were tapping the ground with their thin tiny feet. Their hair was white, their eyes yellow, and their nostrils black. Elga was astonished.

"Where are you from?" she asked the little dogs.

And they answered:

"Do you really not know, Elga? Soldiga made us."

Elga looked, and in place of the toy dogs there stood in front of her live ones, real ones. They had heard the crying of their mistress and come to life.

Elga harnessed her little dogs to a sled and sat on it. The little dogs darted off at a gallop. The forest is not a forest; the river is not a river—the dogs flew straight ahead! Elga closed her eyes. The little dogs had already reached the clouds. When she opened her eyes, Elga saw light all around her . . . Clouds, like fluffy snow, were all around her. Elga took the reins and started to ride the sled.

"Mush-mush-mush!" she cried out. "Hike-hike-hike!"

Only wisps of clouds flew from under the feet of the dogs. Elga did not have time to get tired or to freeze, so quickly had the dogs rushed her to the Anyuy camp.

Elga got off the sled and found the house of Puninga's grandmother. Inside, the old woman lay sick and unwashed, her hair uncombed. Elga, taking pity on her, washed her and combed her hair. She found a ginseng rootlet and gave it to grandmother to chew. After the old one had eaten the rootlet and regained her health, she said to Elga:

"Thank you, my little girl! You're so good! You've done me so much good. And I will pay you back with goodness. It's not the needle my granddaughter wants; it's your death. Your stepmother desires your death. I'll give you a needle. But remember, when you give Puninga the needle, hold it with its eye toward you."

Before the sun had risen from the sea, Elga and her little dogs had returned home.

The bad, terribly bad, stepmother was sitting there.

"Well," she asked, "where is my needle?"

"Here it is," Elga said. "Here's the needle."

She began to give the needle to her stepmother. Then, remembering what the old woman had told her, she turned the eye of the needle toward herself, with its point facing her stepmother.

As soon as Puninga took it in her hand, the needle began to go through her fingers, piercing them, and sewing them together. As much as Puninga tried, she could not separate her fingers.

"Well, you've outsmarted me, you little girl!" she said to Elga.

Suddenly it came to her who was helping Elga. She waited until Elga had fallen asleep. She lit a fire. She threw into the fire all the toys that Elga's father had made. She threw in the reindeer; she threw in the little dogs. They began to burn. Only one little dog jumped from the fire. It ran to Elga and awakened her with its nose:

"Things are bad, Elga! Your stepmother wants to kill us all! Let's run away!"

"Where are we to run?" asked Elga.

"We have to run to where there is no stepmother," answered the little dog.

Elga jumped out of the *yurta* and the little dog jumped right after her.

Puninga saw this and ran after them.

The moon rose, and its path stretched over the river. Elga and the little dog ran on that narrow path, running as if on ice. Puninga rushed after them, but the path broke under her—it could not hold her. The stepmother fell down. But she managed to grasp Elga's small spear and throw it at Elga. When the spear reached Soldiga's daughter, it said to her:

"Forgive me, my little mistress! Now we must part!"

The spear turned around. It flew to the stepmother. The spear entered one of Puninga's eye sockets and came out the other—and turned to dust. Then something strange began to happen. Puninga's eyes grew as big as saucers. Puninga waved her arms—and they became wings. Long claws grew on her feet. Puninga had become a goggle-eyed owl. She wanted to return home, but the wings took her to the *taiga*. The stepmother sat on a tree and cried out:

"Pu-nin-ga! Pu-nin-ga!"

And the owls cry like that to this day.

Elga, with her little dog beside her, ran and ran on the moon's path until they reached the moon. The little girl wanted to go back to the earth, but when it started to get light, the path disappeared, and morning came. So the girl and her little dog remained on the moon.

To this day, Elga descends to the earth on the moon's path, before morning comes. She visits every dwelling, seeking Soldiga's spear; she looks everywhere. She looks at all the weapons to see if Soldiga's spear is there. When she sees a sleeping child with tearful eyes, Elga wipes the tears away and gives the child a pleasant dream, so that the child will forget those fears. And that's why children don't remember fears.

But just before sunrise, when the owl in the *taiga* cries out: "Pu-nin-ga! Pu-nin-ga!" Elga quickly returns to the moon.

You can see her in the night if you open your eyes, when the moon's light touches them.

And that is the end of the tale.

Connect to Your Life
Think of someone you know or have read about who has courageously protected others or stood for equal rights. What risks did he or she take? What dreams or ideas made this person take these risks?

THE GREEDY KANCHUGA

It was the time when animals could still understand human language. Back then, the tiger was a relative of the Udegey people. Back then, the tiger was a welcome visitor to the Bisanka village.

The Bisanka people lived at the headwaters of the Koppi River. Their numbers were many. When they all talked at once, you could hear them all along the Anyuy River.

One year, the hunting was very good. The hunters took in more sables, squirrels, polecats, weasels, bears, and foxes than they ever had before.

Traders came to Bisanka and sold all their goods, but the Bisanka people still had plenty of fur pelts.

The Bisanka people gathered at the Amur River to sell their pelts. They loaded twenty sleds. They harnessed the best dogs in the camp. They put on their best clothing. They entwined new red lace into their braids. They put on caps made of the hide of musk-deer, with sable tails atop them. They tied white *bogdo*—scarves—on their heads. They put on white overalls sewn with silk thread, and they put on white breeches. They sat on the sleds, waved with the driving poles, then placed them between the runners and let the dogs have their own way.

"Mush-mush-mush! Hike-hike-hike!"

The dogs started running. The snow flew to the sides of the creaking runners.

The little dogs barked as they ran. All the wild animals scattered before them and hid in the trees and the snowdrifts, as the dogs flew on like the wind.

The little dogs were so good that they ran without stopping, gulping down *yukola*[20] on the run . . .

The little dogs crossed over mountain ranges; they thought nothing of it. Over mountains, rivers, ravines—the dogs rushed on in a straight line. They reached the headwaters of the Anyuy, then ran on to the Khor, the Ussuri, and finally to the Amur River. How long the Udegeys traveled—who knows? But they traveled happily, not caring about time.

In Mullaki, on the Amur River, the market was a big one. People gathered there from every quarter: the Nanays from the Amur with red ribbons plaited in their braids;

---

20 *Yukola* is a split and sun-dried salmon. After the fish is split lengthwise, the head and backbone is fed to dogs. The meat of the two sides joined by the tail is reserved for human consumption. The fish are dry-cured on a *yukolnik* (a drying rack). *Yukola* is prepared and stored for winter consumption.

The Greedy Kanchuga

the Nivkhi from the islands in fishskin clothing; the Negidals from the Amgun River with their dogs; the Oroks from faraway pastures in their sheepskin clothing; the Ulchi in their moose-deer high boots; the Orochi with their furry high boots of deerskin . . . Really, it's impossible to recount them all!

The market was a big one.

Many traders arrived: braided Manchurians,[21] cleanshaven people with long fingernails; and from islands beyond the sea, traders in wooden *latakh*-boats with two-handed swords.

But with the traders came the black plague.[22] Who brought it first—who knows? Whether it came on a boat, with the little dogs, with the reindeer, on foot—who knows? How it was dressed—who knows? But once it arrived, it became the mistress of the big market.

The Bisanka people started trading, and then—what misfortune!

They were struck by the black plague. And they began to die. The Udegeys, Nanays, Nikans,[23] Negidals, Oroks, Nivkhi, Manchurians, Orochi, and Ulchi—all began to die.

The people saw how bad things were. Death does not bargain with anyone; it takes all equally in order. The people ran away from death in all directions.

But among the Bisanka people there was no one to run! Only one lad was left among the living. His name was Konga. He had arrived with his brother. But the black plague took his brother. Konga buried his other relatives. And then he thought: "How can I leave my brother in a strange land? Let him come with me. Let him be buried according to our custom. Let him stand before the Master for all the relatives!"

Konga made a large box and put his brother in it.

Konga threw away all his goods—they would do him no good . . . He took his seat on the last harnessed sled, shouted at the dogs, and made haste for home from that cursed place!

Konga rode on and did not look back. He was running from the plague.

But the plague was lying in the box with his brother.

How far Konga went—who knows? First he went along the Ussuri River, then along the Khor, then down the Anyuy, and then over the mountains.

In the mountains, Konga came upon a boulder-strewn clearing. In the clearing lay a tigers' den. Many paths led to the den—paths paved with human bones and fenced in with skulls.

---

21 The term *Manchurian* usually refers to the Manchu of northeastern China, neighboring residents of the Manchuria Province in China.

22 Bubonic fever, a highly infectious and often fatal disease.

23 Over the years, many of the names of these tribes have been anglicized or russified; Nikans is not a commonly used name in the ethnographic and historic literature.

Coming up the tiger path, Konga met a tiger standing there. When the tiger saw Konga, he rolled over on his back and became a man. After the tiger-man greeted Konga, he asked him how was the trading and what was the news?

Konga told the tiger-man of the misery he had endured and the bad news he was carrying with him. The tiger-man shook his head and said:

"Carry on! When you bury your brother, I'll come to cry a little. Your brother was a very good hunter . . ." Then he rolled on his back, became a tiger again, and walked away.

Konga continued on the path. From there to his camp was just a short distance.

The lad arrived. He told his mother and relatives what had happened to him and his brother. His mother opened the box to say goodbye to her son.

When she opened the box, the plague escaped.

The black plague started to walk over the camp.

All the people died.

Only a little brother and sister of Konga remained, along with the *shaman* Kanchuga.[24]

Kanchuga was cowardly and greedy. He never helped anybody with anything. He saw that, besides himself, two children remained alive. He thought: "When death goes away, I'll be the only one left. Why should I help the little children? There would not be enough food for me to last."

He closed the door of Konga's *yurta* and put a log against it. He left the children in the *yurta*. He went to his own *yurta* and closed himself in. He sat there and gobbled away at the food until he was completely full.

At first he did not go out at all. Then his greed seized him.

"Why should the food in the camp be wasted?" Kanchuga thought. "It can't be taken from the dead—that is a sin. Bad spirits guard the food of the dead," Kanchuga said to himself. "Well, so what! There are many of them—and I'm only one. When they start throwing themselves at me they will clash with one another, and they'll forget about me!"

So Kanchuga went to collect the food in the *yurtas* of those who had perished. He collected fermented red cranberries, seal blubber, pickled bear's garlic, dried meat, fermented fish eggs, dried lilies, and bird cherry flat cakes—and he ate them all.

In Konga's *yurta*, the hungry children wept.

---

24 During the Soviet period in Russian history (1917–1991), the atheist Soviet government tolerated, but did not encourage, any form of religious and spiritual belief. Religious and spiritual leaders in Soviet society were viewed as "enemies of the people." Because this folktale was written down and censored during the Soviet era, the *shaman* (a religious and spiritual leader) is portrayed as an antagonist to his people.

Then the tiger came to the camp. He rolled on his back and became a man. He saw that there was no smoke, no people walking about, no sounds of a drum, and no dogs barking—all lay there dead. He had come to cry over Konga's dead brother, and now there would not be tears enough—everyone who would have cried with him was dead.

When the tiger-man heard somebody crying inside Konga's *yurta*, he opened the door and found the children. He took them by the hand. He walked over the camp looking for somebody alive. Nobody responded to his calls.

The tiger-man came to Kanchuga's *yurta*. When he tugged at the door, it did not open. But he could hear somebody inside, shuffling around.

He knocked on the door.

Kanchuga heard the knock. He thought that Konga's young siblings had gotten out of their *yurta* and were coming to ask for food. Kanchuga was filling his mouth, chewing mightily, choking on food. With a full mouth, he cried out:

"Go away! Don't ask! I have nothing to eat myself!"

The tiger-man then said:

"Eh, eh, Kanchuga, you've forgotten the rules of the forest people: you shall help the weak, you shall give to the hungry, and you shall give shelter to the orphans. The Udegeys lived that way. And they will continue to live that way. There is no place for you among simple people! Three times you'll die of fear. Your body will become smaller and your greed altogether bigger. That is what will happen to you until you vanish from sight!"

Having pronounced this curse, the man rolled on his back and turned back into a tiger. He put the children on his back and carried them to the tigers' den.

He said to his relatives:

"These are the children of my grandfather. It's time to feed them."

The tigers began to feed the children. They gave them the best pieces of food. And the children began to grow. They gave the children new names so that the black plague would not follow the traces of the old names and come to their new place. They named the little girl Inga, and the little boy Egda.

Soon the children grew up.

Inga learned how to sew clothing, and Egda became a hunter.

When the time came, the old tiger walked with them on the tiger's path, showed them the ways of simple people, and taught them rules to live by so that everything would turn out right. Then he returned to his den.

And Inga and Egda returned to the people.

They passed by the camp of their father. The path leading to the camp was overgrown with grass. Egda tied a bunch of grass over the path so that people passing by would not stop there.

So, that's what happened to the children.

And here's what happened to Kanchuga:

When the tiger-man pronounced his curse, Kanchuga's nose stretched out, fangs stuck out of his mouth, bristles grew on his back, and his fingers and toes turned to hoofs. Kanchuga became a wild boar. He became smaller, but his greed for food became bigger. He gulped down all the food he could find in the *yurtas*. Then he ran to the *taiga* forest. He ate roots, he gnawed green grass, he scavenged acorns—he stuffed himself! His greed for food was choking him, and he could not eat enough. All day he walked in the *taiga* gulping, crunching, and gnawing. But he could not fill himself. Even in his sleep, he munched, snored heavily, and grated his teeth. He wanted acorns, bird giblets, and all sorts of food. When he awakened, he had to go after food again, but his stomach was always empty!

After they left the tiger-people, Inga and Egda came across Kanchuga in the *taiga*.

When Kanchuga saw the brother and sister, he thought, "I'm going to eat them—I'll be sated then!" He then threw himself at Konga's siblings. But Egda shook his spear—and the wild boar-Kanchuga died of fear.

Kanchuga rolled over on his back and became a lynx. He opened his jaws, bared his teeth, and threw himself at Egda, still wanting to eat him . . . Egda shook his spear again and the lynx-Kanchuga died of fear.

He rolled himself over on his back and became a rat. In body he was smaller, but his greed for food grew. He stared with his red eyes, beat the ground with his thin tail, bared his sharp teeth, and jumped at Egda, thinking, "When I eat him, I'll feel full!" But Egda shook his fist at the rat, and Kanchuga died of fear the third time.

He rolled over on his back and became a wood-boring beetle, the kind of beetle that bores into hundred-year-old pines and turns them into dust or rotten wood. The beetle buzzed, spread his wings, moved his feelers back and forth, and kicked with his feet. He flew at Egda, sat on his forehead, and opened his mouth wide—thinking, for the last time, that he would swallow the lad alive.

At this Egda became angry:

"If your malice does not leave you and your greed does not lessen, blame yourself and not me—so far as you and I are concerned, I am guilty of nothing . . ."

Egda then slapped his forehead, crushing the bug.

So the greedy Kanchuga perished for the last time and final time. Having stolen food from the children, he died by their hand.

And nobody felt sorry for him.

That is all.

Discussion Topics

In the ancient oral narratives, villains, in contrast to more humble heroes, use words and power intentionally to exploit, control, transfix, incarcerate, and destroy for their own gain. Highly individualistic, they hold no respect for nature and other human beings, and actually seek to abuse magic by preventing change and causing everything to be transfixed according to their interests. On the other side, the marvelous protagonist wants to keep the process of natural change flowing and in balance, seeking, often in collaboration with figures from the natural world, to overcome the obstacles that prevent other characters or creatures from living in a peaceful and pleasurable way.

Contrast and compare antagonist and protagonist behavior and intentions in today's global society. Support your arguments with specific examples.

KILE BAMBA AND LOCHE-THE STRONGMAN

In truth, this didn't happen so very long ago. On the Amur River there lived Kile Bamba—a Nanay man with the strength of a strongman.

Kile was born of an ordinary woman. But it seems that his good spirits helped him to grow up quickly. He was already catching wild animals while he was still suckling at his mother's breast.

One day his mother left the house. She put a small log against the door so it would not open. She spent some time visiting the neighbors—who knows how long? While she was gone, a tiger jumped into Bamba's house through an open window.

The neighbors heard the roar of the tiger. Then they heard little Bamba begin to cry. The relatives rushed every which way; why wouldn't they run away, with a tiger in the village?

Bamba cried a little and then became quiet.

"Well," the relatives thought, "the little Bamba is dead. The tiger dragged him into the *taiga*!"

His mother ran back home.

There was Bamba, lying on his back, blowing bubbles from his nose and playing with the tiger's furry tail. The tiger lay next to his cradle—it seems little Bamba had choked him to death. What a Bamba!

When he saw his mother come in, he took the sucking pacifier out of his mouth.

"Well, there's trouble," he said. "There are so many animals that they don't let you sleep, they jump in through the windows! It seems it's up to me to take care of them as long as there are no men in the village!"

Bamba stood up. He took his father's spear in his hands, pondering.

"Not the right size!" he declared.

He grasped the spear with both hands, bent it, and broke it in two.

"It's rather bad!" he said.

He went to the *taiga*, grasped a young larch with his left hand, stepped aside, tore it out of the ground, stripped the twigs off it, and shook the earth from its roots, trying to see if it would do.

"Sort of light!" he said. "But since there's no other, I can do nothing more. It'll have to do."

His relatives watched him with amazement. There had never been such a Nanay. And they did not call him Kile Bamba anymore, but Mergen Bamba—the strongman Bamba.

Bamba then becomes such a good hunter that it is hard to imagine anyone better. As soon as Bamba leaves the house and starts getting ready for the hunt, the animals in their burrows beyond nine mountain ranges and ten lakes take leave of their children, knowing they can't escape from Bamba!

Bamba has keen eyes: he takes one look and right away knows how many silver hairs the silver fox has on her back and how many white ones are on her tail.

Bamba is also keen of hearing: after listening a bit, he'll say, "Beyond nine rivers and nine brooks there are sables chattering. That's where we have to put our traps."

Bamba is strong: for a hundred days he hunts animals without pause; then he sleeps for a night and kills animals for the next hundred days.

Bamba eats a lot: in the morning a roe deer, for dinner an elk, and for supper a bear! He eats them all. Patting his belly, he boasts: "I could eat more, but I have to put something aside for tomorrow!"

Bamba is the only one shooting, but it takes ten hunters to collect the kill. A big procession of sleds follows Bamba when, still a boy, he returns from the hunt; and every sled is piled high with furs. That's Bamba for you!

Bamba is good-natured: when he hears a child crying somewhere in the village, he goes there and says: "Why are you howling? Here is a bunch of flowers for you. Play." Or he gives an inflated fish bladder to the child. The child taps the bladder with his palms; the bladder makes a noise and the child stops crying. Bamba has killed so many bears that he could hang a *mafa garani*—a bear's fang—over the cradle of every child in the village for good luck, so that the evil spirits would not frighten them. Everybody in the village is well fed. There is plenty of meat, plenty of fish, and plenty of furry animals.

One day, the Nanays traveled beyond the river to the realm of the Nikans in Manchuria. They traded their furs with Nikans to procure clothing and supplies.

The Nanays are round-faced; their bellies are big; their eyes are clear; their braids are plaited with red ribbons; their high fur boots are beautifully sewn with silk thread; their hands are deft; and their legs are fast. Such are the Nanays!

From the other bank of the river, the Nikan-*Amban*[25]—leader of the Nikans—looked and looked. He became envious: the Nanays live well, they live in peace and friendship, they pay *yasak*-tribute[26] to nobody . . . they have everything.

---

25 See footnote 18 of this edition.

26 *Yasak* is a payment by the Natives to the Russian officialdoms for permission to use hunting and grazing land.

The *Amban* had fleeced his own peasants to the bone long ago. He took for himself, he took for the realm, he took for the soldiers, he took for the monks, he took for the merchants, and again he took for himself—and so what was left for the peasants? "Let me," thought the *Amban*, "take a *yasak* from the Nanays! I'll take *yasak* from them. I'll make a fortune."

So, to the Nanays he sent his soldiers and officials—an innumerable force! They went there with sabers, spears, and firearms.

This force came to the Nanays, who were glad to have visitors and wanted to host them. But the Nikans didn't even look at the food they were offered. They went directly to raid the storehouses. This angered Bamba.

"You're boors," he said. "You don't know how to behave as guests!"

The soldiers of the Manchu-*Amban* had plaited braids.

Bamba seized the soldiers by their long braids, tied them together, and threw them into the water. The Nikans gurgled in the water, gurgled and drowned . . . Bamba was strong!

The Manchu-*Amban* of the Nikans sent his soldiers several times and they did not come back. The *Amban* then realized that the Amur people could not be taken by force. So he invited all of his wise men to decide how they could gain a profit from the Amur land. The *Amban* and his wise men thought and thought . . . and then they thought some more.

The oldest of the men said to the *Amban*:

"Don't send soldiers; soldiers think with their swords and not with their heads. Send a merchant to the Nanays. A merchant is like a spider; he sticks to the skin and he doesn't let go until he has drunk all of the blood!"

And that's what the *Amban* did. He sent the merchant Li-Chan to the Nanays.

Li-Chan came to the Nanays on the Amur River. Li-Chan was like a fox. His speech was smooth and he promised boxes of goods to every Nanay. Li-Chan's tongue had no bones in it—like the tail of a fox it lay low with the wind. Li-Chan arrived and began to hand out his goods to the Nanays: "Take it, take it! We'll square accounts later!" To some, he'd give beads; to some, kettles; to some, robes decorated with designs; to some earrings; and, to some, cereals with flour. "Take it, take it! We'll square accounts later!" The Nanays saw that he was a good merchant. The Nanays saw that they could live with Li-Chan. The merchant doesn't yell, threaten, or stamp his feet. He does everything with a smile on his face, chuckling all the time.

So the merchant trained the Nanays to get used to him. The Nanays no longer traveled to the country of the Nikans, and no longer brought back goods. They could buy anything they needed from Li-Chan; anything they asked for, the merchant had it.

Then the time came to pay Li-Chan.

The Nanays brought their furs to Li-Chan.

Suddenly everything they had purchased from the merchant had become very expensive. Li-Chan said to them:

"The road is a difficult one, the goods have to be brought in, the robbers on the road are unrestrained, one has to pay the *Amban*, the robbers have to be paid off, the Nikans' ruler has to be paid."

The Nanays gave him all of their furs, but the furs did not cover the debt. The Nanays stayed in debt to Li-Chan. But the Nanays are the sort of people who believe that debt should be paid! So the Nanays started working to pay off what they owed. What they got from the *taiga*—Li-Chan took. What they caught in the water went to him, too. Li-Chan, who had come to the Nanays as thin as a worm, was now as fat as a hog! In the meantime, the Nanays got skinny. They could not work off the debt in any way . . .

They thought and thought. Finally, they went to Kile Bamba . . .

"This is what's wrong," they sighed. "In no way can we pay our debts. It seems that a devil is involved in this. In the beginning, Li-Chan counted two pelts as one. And now Li-Chan counts three pelts as one. How can this be?"

Bamba went to the merchant. He was angry. He asked the merchant how can this be. Li-Chan showed him his ledger—a book in which he entered his debts and accounts. Bamba looked—he did not understand the marks that were entered in the book, but he did see that, in truth, they were there. If there are as many debts as there are marks, the Nanays would never rid themselves of the debts. Bamba did not realize that there were more false entries than debts.

Bamba began to ask the Nanays what they had received from Li-Chan. They answered, "I took a robe, I took cereals, I took vodka . . . and what happened after that—I don't know!" The Nanays remembered what they got before they drank vodka, but did not remember anything after drinking it. The vodka had knocked all the memory out of their heads.

Bamba started to help his kin.

He did not rid them of their poverty, but became poor himself, and seemingly fell in debt to Li-Chan. How this happened, Bamba did not know.

"It seems that Li-Chan is not a merchant, but a devil," thought Bamba. "I cannot understand why three pelts are equal to one!"

Bamba went to a *shaman* to ask about the merchant. But the *shaman* sat there drunk, overly drunk, and barely able to move his tongue. He listened to Bamba. He listened, then he said:

"You're right! Li-Chan is a devil! Look here at what kind of vodka he gave me. Three days ago I drank it and to this day I'm drunk. Is it possible that a simple man could do such a thing? To be sure, Li-Chan is a devil!"

"Well, and what can a hunter do against a devil? Nothing . . ."

Bamba said to the *shaman*:

"Shamanize a little! Drive that devil Li-Chan away! The Nanays are wasting away; they have to give all their food to him. Soon they'll begin to die!"

The *shaman* replied:

"I cannot shamanize against Li-Chan. He is the kind of devil I can't cope with. He's not a Nanay, but a Nikan devil! He is an *Amba-Amban*, a devil's devil! You'd better give him the furry animals."

"I'm going to hunt animals in the forbidden forest," said Bamba. "I'm going to the Sikhote-Alin Mountains to hunt for the tiger, snow leopard, and lynx!"

"You can't go there," the *shaman* said. "Hunt around here. The mountain devils live in the Sikhote-Alin. The Udegey Kakzamu guards those mountains; he turns people into stone."

"I'll go to the Big Sea! I'll hunt for the sea lion, walrus, and seal there," Bamba said.

The *shaman* waved his hands at him.

"Hunt around here! The water devil, Ganka, lives in the Big Sea. He has a human trunk, he has a fish's tail, and he's got an iron hook for a hand. He sticks his hook out of the water and grabs people with it!"

"I'll go to the marsh! I'll hunt for the bittern, egret, and mallard," Bamba said.

The *shaman* sputtered:

"You hunt here, I'm telling you! The devil Boko lives in the marsh; he has one leg only. He'll lead you into the marsh and leave you in a quagmire. You'll drown there, blowing bubbles to the surface until you suffocate."

"Then I'll go to the barrens with salt lakes," said Bamba. "I'll hunt the antlered elk!"

The *shaman* was shaking in anger.

"I'm telling you, you hunt here! On the barrens with salt lakes lives Agdy-Thunder. He fells trees with the stone axe. When he hits a man—that man turns to dust!"

"I'll go to the Milka Lake and kill beavers and ducks!"

The *shaman's* mouth was foaming with anger at Bamba:

"Khimu-*amban*, the most terrifying of the devils, lives in that lake. When he sees a man, he crawls out of the lake, and the grass and stones under him catch on fire! Khimu will breathe fire on you; you'll burn, and nobody will know of it!"

Mergen Bamba lowered his head. He started thinking: "But Bamba, you are a strongman! There are devils all around you. And all are stronger than I—Mergen Bamba. I can't use my strength. Oy-yakha! Woe to me! Everything is bad . . ."

"Hunt as you hunted before," the *shaman* advised, "but give the pelts to Li-Chan. He'll give you vodka and you'll forget your miseries."

Bamba did not want to go to Li-Chan. He went wherever his eyes took him . . .

He jumped over three brooks, he walked around six lakes, and he climbed over nine mountains. He selected a place, built a shelter of branches, and lit a fire. He started to think hard: "Why does a man have the power of a strongman when his life depends on devils? It's not enough that there are devils in the forest, devils in the mountains, devils in the river! Now there's the devil Li-Chan in the village! Where could one find such strength that he could defeat all of the devils so that people could live well again?"

Kile Bamba fell asleep. He slept. He awoke when he heard that somebody was coming from the headwaters of the Amur River—someone with steps so heavy he weighed down the *taiga* soil, squeezing water out of it. Bamba jumped up, put an arrow on the bowstring, and took out his knife.

"Who is that coming?" Bamba wondered.

A man walked out from behind the trees. Bamba had never seen such a man before: a white face, blue eyes, yellow hair—like gold—a long beard. His clothes were not those of an Amur man. In his hands, he held a kind of iron stick that Bamba did not recognize.

"Another devil has come here!" Bamba thought.

The man spoke to him:

"Why are you holding your bow that way? Maybe you want to shoot me? Let's compete with each other and see who can shoot farther."

What strongman would avoid an argument?

Bamba put on a dignified air—in the village nobody could shoot farther than he could! He saw a hare running beyond three brooks. He loosed an arrow and impaled the hare onto a pine tree.

"Very good!" said the man with the yellow hair, as he shouldered his iron stick.

"Beyond six brooks," he said, "right now, there is a squirrel who is about to jump from tree to tree—I'll kill it in flight."

He took aim with his stick, narrowed his blue eyes. Something seemed to crash—like thunder rolling over the mountains!

Kile Bamba fell to the ground, frightened.

"Oy, Ardy-Thunder," he pleaded, "don't strike me!"

"That's not Ardy—it's me," the man laughed.

Bamba looked. The squirrel was already lying on its side!

"You have the upper hand," Bamba said. "Let's wrestle."

They took off their clothes; they grasped each other at the waist. They began to wrestle. Neither could overcome the other. Neither could wrestle the other to the ground. Bamba tried to manage throwing that man over his back, but the man lifted Bamba into the air and did not let him down. He held him up there, he held him . . .

Bamba's eyes clouded, as he pleaded:

"Put me down, I'm not a bird. Without ground under my feet, I'm no good. You have the upper hand . . . Let's see who dances better."

The man set him down. Bamba started to dance. He began in the morning and did not stop dancing until the sun set. Never had anybody on the Amur danced like that!

The man grunted, spat on the palms of his hands, and took his turn. He danced through the night and through the next day; the second night came and he danced all through it... Then a hissing was heard in the valley, and a great noise from the stomping of his feet: the water splashed out of the rivers, the earth shook, and columns of dust covered the stars...

"All right, pal," Bamba cried out, "that's enough. It's all yours!"

But the man danced yet for three days and three nights, clapping his heels with the palms of his hands. After he stopped, he said:

"That wasn't a dance! When I was young, I used to dance!"

"Would a bad man be able to dance like that?" wondered Bamba. "His arms are strong, his eyes are alert, and his temper is a happy one—why not be a pal to him?"

They became like sworn brothers.

"I'm Kile Bamba," said the Nanay.

"I'm Ivan Russkiy,[27] but in your language, Loche."

"Are you a strongman in your land?" Bamba asked.

Loche waved his arm.

"What do you mean, strongman?" he said. "There are strongmen there, but I'm simply the youngest son of my dear mother."

"What did you come here for?" Bamba asked.

"I'm going to live here. My ancestors lived on this land long ago."

"It's bad around here," warned the Nanay.

"What? Is the land bad?" Ivan asked.

He took a lump of soil, spread it over his palm, and smelled it:

"The earth is good!"

"There are many devils about," Bamba said. "They don't let you live!"

Bamba told Ivan about his troubles—how the devils entangled his arms and legs, depriving him of his strength.

"Don't worry," Ivan said, "as long as there's light in your eyes, you can always keep the devil in line!"

---

27 Ivan the Russian.

Then they went to the village. The Nanays were milling around, looking pallid—there was nothing to eat. Only Li-Chan sat at the entrance of the path to his house—fat and red like a tick.

"The one over there, is he a devil?" Ivan asked.

"That's the one, that's the one!"

Ivan and Bamba went to the storehouses. The storehouses were empty. There was a spider's web in a corner of one of them. Ivan took the web and rolled it into a lump. He went to Li-Chan.

"Let me have the ledger—the book," he said. "Where is it written how much my companion Bamba owes you?"

Li-Chan got hold of the book, opened it, and with a thick finger jabbed at something.

Ivan took the book and said:

"If Bamba really owes you, if these words are true, the book will not burn in the fire! If you have cheated Bamba—your words will burn!"

He threw the book in the fire. The book caught fire right away and burned up. Li-Chan started to yell, stamping his feet before Ivan. Ivan took the lump of spider's web that he had gathered in the Nanay storehouse and threw it into Li-Chan's mouth. Li-Chan grew thin right away, withered, became small, and turned into a spider. Ivan threw him in the river and Li-Chan swam to Manchu-*Amban*, his leader.

The Nanays were walking around hungry.

Ivan plucked from his chest a number of small seeds and threw them on the ground. Immediately green grass sprang up and became yellow. The ears of the grass were swollen with small, yellow seedlets. Ivan took the seedlets, ground them between stones, and made a white powder. He mixed the powder with water from the Amur and made dough. With the dough he made flat cakes and baked them. He gave them to the Nanays, "Eat these!"

The Nanays ate the cakes. They were tasty. The Nanays gained more strength than they had ever gained from a meal before.

The Nanays went hunting.

Bamba and Ivan also went hunting.

"I want to kill an elk," Ivan said. "Let's go to the barrens and lakes!"

"But Ardy-Thunder lives there," said Bamba.

Ivan was unimpressed.

"How can you desert your sworn brother?" Bamba asked himself. "You'd lose face!"

So Bamba went with him. Ivan started shooting with his rifle. He made such a thunderous noise that Ardy flew away from the barrens.

"This is a good place to hunt," Ivan said. "And where is your Ardy?"

The sworn brothers went farther. They went into the marsh. Bamba saw a small hunchbacked man standing on the path. He had only one leg, and his eyes were burning with a blue fire.

"Don't go to him, Ivan!" Bamba cried out. "It's the hunchback Boko—a devil. He'll mislead you, destroy you!"

Ivan questioned:

"What kind of a devil is Boko?" and he grasped Boko by his single leg and threw him under his feet so that Bamba and Ivan could cross the quagmire.

Then Bamba saw that Boko was not lying there, only a spruce twig was lying there. "Maybe there never was a Boko!" he thought to himself.

Next, they were about to cross a river, when Bamba became troubled by the sight of gray disheveled locks and green eyes sparkling in the water.

"Don't go in the river!" Bamba warned Ivan. "Look, the old man Ganka is lying in the water! He's lying in wait for us! Look, he's put out his iron hand!"

But Ivan dove in the water and grabbed that gray devil! When he jumped out, he was holding in his hands a snagged pine tree and the large-toothed pike that had been swimming under the tree. Ivan and Bamba ate the pike and continued on. And Bamba never again saw the devil Ganka.

The sworn brothers went over the mountains. Bamba was trembling from fear—they were going through the places where Kakzamu lies in wait for people. As soon as Bamba started thinking about Kakzamu, there he was, right there. With his red eyes he stares at people, gets hold of them, and turns them to stone . . .

"Ivan!" Bamba cried out. "Let's run from here! Run on grass! Kakzamu will have no power over us if we run on grass!"

Ivan glanced back—and how he did take care of Kakzamu with his iron stick! How the sparks flew, flew in every direction! Kakzamu's eyes closed . . . Bamba looked—and there was a gray boulder covered with moss. There wasn't a sign of Kakzamu. "He hid himself," thought Bamba. Bamba walked behind Ivan. He looked back. There was no Kakzamu; that was the last of him! He perished from Ivan's blows.

"Well, where does your devil Khimu live?" Ivan asked Bamba.

Ivan had barely finished asking the question, when the brothers came to a lake out of which Khimu crept toward them—wriggling, coiling, and breathing fire. Bamba yelled out. He wanted to run away. But Ivan questioned him:

"What's with you, Bamba? Haven't you ever seen a brush fire?"

Bamba turned around—there was no Khimu and he probably never existed.

True enough, the grass was burning and the fire, like a snake, was creeping throughout the land. True enough, the stones around them were lying like fish scales. But there was no Khimu! Bamba sighed with relief.

Bamba now saw that there were no devils, and that he and Ivan were standing on Native land. Both were free, both were brave, both were strongmen—only Ivan was somewhat older. And around them everything was quite natural—in the forest trees were growing, animals lived in the *taiga*, fish were swimming in the river, and there were boulders in the mountains. Bamba thought and thought, then suddenly exclaimed:

"All this means that our tales have vanished! About the *taiga*-people, the water-people, and the mountain-people—the tales have vanished."

"But Bamba," said Ivan, "other tales, not unlike the old ones, will come to be. Really, aren't you strong? Aren't you brave? Aren't you master of your own land? And am I not your friend? Really, aren't people always going to tell tales about us?"

From then on new tales would be told—tales about love and friendship, tales about strength and courage, and tales about deftness and fidelity. New tales would be told about stoutheartedness, strong arms, and true vision.

That's the whole story.

Discussion Topics

Can one land ever really be home to more than one people? To native and newcomer, for instance? Or to Arab and Jew, Hutu and Tutsi, Albanian and Kosovor, Turk and Kurd? Can the world ever be home to all of Us? Will a time come when the human race will move beyond the "Them and Us" concept in order to achieve harmonious and peaceful coexistence on Planet Earth?

Share your ideas about future possibilities for peaceful coexistence. If you think it is possible for one land to be home to more than one people, explain why you think so. Or, if you think the time will not come when the earth's peoples will live together in harmony, explain why you think not.

SUGGESTED BIBLIOGRAPHY

Folktale Collections and Related Literature

Andersen, Hans Christian
    1974   *The Complete Fairy Tales and Stories.* Trans. Eric Christian Haugaard. New York: Doubleday.

de Laguna, Frederica and Dale DeArmond
    1995   *Tales from the Dena: Indian Stories from the Tanana, Koyukuk, & Yukon Rivers.* Seattle & London: University of Washington Press.

Dolitsky, Alexander B. and Henry N. Michael (eds.)
    1997   *Fairy Tales and Myths of the Bering Strait Chukchi.* Juneau: Alaska-Siberia Research Center, Publication No. 9.

    2000   *Tales and Legends of the Yupik Eskimos of Siberia.* Juneau: Alaska-Siberia Research Center, Publication No. 11.

    2002   *Ancient Tales of Kamchatka.* Juneau: Alaska-Siberia Research Center, Publication No. 12.

Grimm, Jacob and Wilhelm
    1987   *The Complete Fairy Tales of the Brothers Grimm. Ed. and Trans. Jack Zipes.* New York: Bantam.

Luthi, Max
    1982   *The European Folktale: Form and Nature.* Bloomington & Indianapolis: Indiana University Press.

Nagishkin, Dmitriy
    1980   *Amurskiye Skazki* [*Fairy Tales of the Amur*]. Khabarovsk: Khabarovsk Press, Russia.

Zipes, Jack (ed.)
    2001   *The Great Fairy Tale Tradition: From Straparola and Basile to the Brothers Grimm.* New York & London: W.W. Norton & Company.

Wildlife Manuscripts and Related Literature

Matthiessen, Peter and Maurice Hornocker
    2001   *Tigers in the Snow.* North Point Press.

Nowak, M. Ronald
    1999   *Walker's Mammals of the World.* John Hopkins University Press.

Prynn, David
    2002   *Amur Tiger.* Russian Nature Press.

Rabinowitz, Alan
    2008   *Life in the Valley of Death: The Fight to Save Tigers in a Land of Guns, Gold, and Greed.* Washington, Covelo, London: Island Press.

Sunquist, Mel and Fiona Sunquist
    2002   *Wild Cats of the World.* Chicago: University of Chicago Press.

Thapar, Valmik
    2003   *Tiger: The Ultimate Guide.* CDS Books.

Turner, Alan and Mauricio Anton
    1997   *The Big Cats and Their Fossil Relatives.* New York: Columbia University Press.

GLOSSARY

Amban An evil spirit in the spiritual beliefs of the indigenous peoples of the Amur area.

Autonomous oblast This administrative unit is based on the nature of the economy and composition of Native people of the unit. In the pre-*glasnost* period (before 1985), each *autonomous oblast* was represented in the Soviet of Nationalities of the Supreme Soviet of the Union of Soviet Socialist Republics by five deputies. The executive, administrative, and judicial procedures within an *autonomous oblast* are carried out in the language of the local nationality.

Cossacks [pl.] Free Russian peasants commonly recruited by the tsar's government to serve in the army. Because Russian *Cossacks* were among the first explorers of Siberia, the Russian Far East, and North America in the seventeenth and eighteenth centuries, aboriginal people of the Russian Far North and North America have long been using this word to describe a white man.

Egalitarian society One that gives equal rights to all people; it usually results in sharing and cooperation.

Kray A large administrative and territorial unit, which supersedes the *oblast* and *rayon* districts. The literal meaning of *kray* in the Slavic languages is "edge," reflecting the original pioneering nature of the *krays*. There were nine *krays* in the territory of the former Soviet Union: six in the Russian Federation and three in Kazakhstan.

Manchurian This term usually refers to the Manchu of northeastern China, residents of the Manchuria Province.

Narty [pl.] Sleds pulled by harnessed dogs or deer, used throughout northern Russia for travel.

National okrug One of the territorial designations through which the autonomy of small nationalities is effected. In the 1920s and 1930s, *national okrugs* were established in *krays* and *oblasts* within the territory of the former Russian Soviet Federated Socialist Republic.

Oblast An administrative district not containing an autonomous area. The 1977 constitution of the former Union of Soviet Socialist Republics assigned the resolution of problems concerning *oblast* and *kray* administrative and territorial units to the governments of each former Soviet republic. Where an autonomous area peopled mainly by a national minority exists as an enclave within the district, the proper term is *kray*. The governing body of an *oblast* was the *Oblast* Soviet Deputies of the Working People. (See also *autonomous oblast*.)

Okrug A tier of councils termed the *Okrug Soviet* in the early days of the Soviet Union. *Okrug* roughly corresponded to the old *volost*, or rural district in which both village soviets and city soviets were represented. (*See* also *national okrug*.)

Paleoasiatic A term coined by S. Schrenk (Shrenk), a Russian ethnographer in the mid-nineteenth century. Under this term, he grouped, on the basis of languages, several Siberian and Far East peoples, among them Yukaghirs, Koryaks, Chukchi, Asiatic Eskimos, Kereks, Itelmen, Kets, Nivkhi, and Ainu. Today, the term *Paleoasiatic*, used only with great caution, is normally avoided by North American scholars.

Rayon An administrative district of an *oblast*. *Rayon* is an urban area, formed mainly on lines of economic production, comprising a number of adjacent villages and hamlets, together with small cities (*posyolki*) and other urban settlements found in the area. The geographic size and population of a *rayon* differ according to local circumstances; normally a *rayon* is smaller in size than an *oblast*, *kray*, or *orkug*.

Shaman A Russian word from the Tungus language that anthropologists commonly ascribe to a village spiritual leader or healer. According to the religious ideas of many northern peoples, the *shaman* was a person chosen by spirits and other supernatural creatures to fill the role of intermediary between people and the other worlds.

Sven A common spirit in the spiritual beliefs of the indigenous peoples of the Amur area.

Taiga The Russian term for a dense marshy forest in the northern hemisphere.

Yasak A payment by the Natives to the Russian officials in the seventeenth and eighteenth centuries, made in exchange for permission to use hunting and grazing lands.

Yukola Split and sun-dried salmon. The fish would be split lengthwise, with the head and backbone fed to dogs; the meat of the two sides joined by the tail would be reserved for human consumption. The fish were dry-cured on a *yukolnik*, a drying rack, and stored for winter consumption.

Yurta A tent used by Siberian nomads as a shelter. Made of felt stretched over a light wood framework and able to be disassembled in less than an hour, it has been called the best portable dwelling developed by man. The *yurta* is cylindrical with a dome top. A wattle wall about five feet high is topped with a wooden frame for the dome. Inside, carpets cover the bare earth.

ABOUT THE EDITOR

Alexander B. Dolitsky was born and raised in Kiev in the former Soviet Union. He received an M.A. in history from Kiev Pedagogical Institute, Ukraine, in 1976; an M.A. in anthropology and archaeology from Brown University in 1983; and attended the Ph.D. program in anthropology at Bryn Mawr College from 1983 to 1985, where he was also a lecturer in the Russian Center. In the Union of Soviet Socialist Republics, he was a social studies teacher for three years, and an archaeologist for five years for the Ukranian Academy of Sciences. In 1978, he settled in the United States. Dolitsky visited Alaska for the first time in 1981, while conducting field research for graduate school at Brown. He lived first in Sitka in 1985 and then settled in Juneau in 1986. From 1985 to 1987, he worked as a U.S. Forest Service archaeologist and social scientist. He was an Adjunct Assistant Professor of Russian Studies at the University of Alaska Southeast from 1985 to 1999; Social Studies Instructor at the Alyeska Central School, Alaska Department of Education from 1988 to 2006; and has been the Director of the Alaska-Siberia Research Center (*see* www.aksrc.org) from 1990 to the present. He has conducted about thirty field studies in various areas of the former Soviet Union, Central Asia, South America, Eastern Europe, and the United States. Dolitsky has been a lecturer on the *World Discoverer* and *Spirit of Oceanus* vessels in the Arctic and sub-Arctic regions. He was the Project Manager for the WWII Alaska-Siberia Lend-Lease Memorial, erected in Fairbanks in 2006. Dolitsky has published extensively in the fields of anthropology, history, archaeology, and ethnography in *Current Anthropology, American Antiquity, Arctic, Ultimate Reality and Meaning, Bulletin of Archaeology and Art History,* and *Sibirica.* His more recent books include *Fairy Tales and Myths of the Bering Strait Chukchi* (1997), *Tales and Legends of the Yupik Eskimos of Siberia* (2000), *Ancient Tales of Kamchatka* (2002), *Old Russia in Modern America: Russian Old Believers in Alaska* (1998, 2007), and *Allies in Wartime: The Alaska-Siberia Airway During World War II* (2007). He is working on a book titled *Ancient Tales of Siberia: Nganasans.* In November 2007, Dolitsky was nominated for the *Russian Compatriot of the Year* award in the United States of America.

ABOUT THE TRANSLATOR

Henry N. Michael (1913–2006) was born in Pittsburgh in 1913, but grew up in Prague, Czechoslovakia. He returned to Pennsylvania in the early 1930s. From 1942 to 1945, during World War II, he served in the Armed Forces as a first lieutenant in Europe. He earned his Ph.D. from the University of Pennsylvania in 1954, with a dissertation on *The Neolithic Age in Eastern Siberia*. His interest in the Arctic and sub-Arctic regions was long standing. His ground-breaking work in the application of tree-ring analysis revolutionized archaeological dating techniques. His work would result in a method of correcting radiocarbon-dating techniques discovered by Nobel laureate Willard Libby in 1949. Over the years, Michael published extensively on various aspects of the archaeology, dendrachronology, and ethnography of the Far North. As director and editor of the series *Anthropology of the North: Translations from Russian Sources* (1959–1974), he published several books of translated works. These include S.I. Rudenko's *The Ancient Culture of the Bering Sea and the Eskimo Problem* (1961), and *Studies in Siberian Ethnogenesis* (1962); M.G. Levin's *Ethnic Origins of the People of Northeastern Asia* (1963); the much-quoted *Studies in Siberian Shamanism* (1963); and *Lieutenant Zagoskin's Travels in Russian America* (1967). He also translated M. Levin's and P. Potapov's *Historico-Ethnographic Atlas of Siberia* (in preparation for printing), Menovshchikov's *Fairy Tales and Myths of the Bering Strait Chukchi* (1997), *Tales and Legends of the Yupik Eskimos of Siberia* (2000), *Ancient Tales of Kamchatka* (2002), and several others. From 1948 to 1980, Michael taught first at the University of Pennsylvania and then at Temple University in Philadelphia. He was associated for more than half a century with the University Museum at the University of Pennsylvania. In April of 2000, the University Museum awarded Dr. Michael with the Director's Award, established by the Penn Museum to honor exceptional volunteer achievement.

CONTRIBUTORS

William Blake (1757–1827) was an English artist, mystic, and poet who wrote *Songs of Innocence* (1789), a series of poems celebrating the innocent child's spontaneous and wondrous experience of nature. In addition to "The Tyger," the series includes such well-known poems as "Little Boy Lost," "Little Boy Found," and "The Lamb." U.K.

Alexander B. Dolitsky is the Chairman of the Alaska-Siberia Research Center. He was born and raised in Kiev in the former Soviet Union (*see* About the Editor). U.S.A.

Dr. Henry N. Michael (1913–2006) was born in Pittsburgh and grew up in Prague, Czechoslovakia (*see* About the Translator). U.S.A.

Jason Morgan is an accomplished wildlife artist who lives and works in the United Kingdom, and whose prints and original paintings can be found in collections worldwide. He is a Signature member of the Artists for Conservation Foundation. U.K.

Dmitriy Nagishkin (1909–1961) was born in Chita in southwestern Siberia. In the 1920s and 1930s, Nagishkin published several literary essays in local newspapers. Over the years, he worked as a graphic designer for various publishers. His first literary fairy tales were published in 1938, and he soon thereafter received wide recognition in the former Soviet Union. He wrote down the well-known tales *The Little Boy Chokcho* (1945), *Fairy Tales of the Amur* (1946, 1980), and *Courageous Azmun* (1949). He also published several works of fiction, including *The Heart of the Bonivur* (1953), a historical fiction novel about the Civil War in the Russian Far East in the early 1920s. Nagishkin's books have been translated and published in many world languages. Russia.

Wallace M. Olson is a Professor of Anthropology (Emeritus), University of Alaska Southeast, Juneau, Alaska. U.S.A.

Gennadiy Pavlishin is a prominent book illustrator. He was born in 1938 in Khabarovsk, in the Russian Far East, where he still lives with his two daughters, who actively assist him in his creative work. Russia.

Gordon J.L. Ramel is a frequently-published poet who also holds a master's degree in the Ecology of Soil Arthropods from the University of Exeter in the United Kingdom. U.K.

INDEX

A
Ainu, 6, 66
amban, 8, 30, 31, 33, 50, 51, 52, 54, 58, 65
Amur River estuary, 2
Amur River, 5, 6, 8, 9, 39, 40, 47, 51, 55
Amur tiger, 64
Amur-Ussuri region, 6, 9
animism, xi
Anyuy River, 34, 36, 39, 41
Ardy-Thunder, 55, 58
Autonomous *oblast*, 65

B
Bamba, xii, 2, 47–48, 50–52, 54–56, 58–59, 61
bear, xi–xiii, 11, 12, 17, 39, 43, 50
beaver, xi, 54
Bisanka village, 39
Blake, William, 13, 14, 71
bogdo, 39
Boko, 24, 54, 59
Brown, Steve, xiii
butterflies, xi

C
canoe, xiii
China, 12, 41, 65
Chinese merchants, 2
Chukchi, 6, 63, 66, 67, 69
cosmology, xii
Cossacks, 2, 65
coyotes, xi

D
DeArmond, Dale, 63
deer, 11, 39, 41, 50, 65

de Laguna, Frederica, 63
Dodd, Liz, ix
Dolitsky, Alexander B., ix, 3, 8, 12, 63, 67, 71

E
eagle, xi, xiii, 21, 22, 24, 25, 27
Eastern Orthodox, 8
egalitarian society, 2, 65
Egda, 44, 45
Elga, xii, 2, 29, 30, 31, 33, 34, 36, 37
Evenk, 5

F
fairy tales, ix, 63, 67, 69, 71
folklore, 1
folktales, ix, xi–xiii, 1–3, 43, 63
frog, xi, xiii, 21

G
Ganka, 54, 59
Gomes, John, ix
gorilla, xii, xiii
greed, 2, 15, 43–45, 64
Grimm, Jacob and William, xii, 63

H
Hahn, Jeffrey, ix, 63
hare's heart, 1, 19, 27, 28
Head Canoe, xiii

I
Indiga, 1, 2, 17, 18, 19, 21, 22, 24, 25, 27, 28
Inga, 44, 45
Ivan, 2, 56, 58, 59, 61

J
Jason Morgan (under Morgan, Jason)

K
Kakzamu, 25, 27, 54, 59
Kanchuga, xii, 2, 39, 43–45
Khabarovsk *Kray*, 6, 9
Khimu-*amban*, 54
Kile Bamba, xii, 2, 47, 50, 52, 55, 56
killer whale, xiii
Kolkhorst Ruddy, Kathy, ix
Konga, 41, 43, 44, 45
Koppi River, 17, 39
Korea, 9, 12
kray, 6, 9, 65, 66

L
Lancaster, Miriam, ix
ledger-book, 52, 58
Li-Chan, 2, 51, 52, 54, 55, 58
Lightbourne, Inc., ix
Loche-The Strong Man, xii, 2, 47
Longyear, Willis, ix
lynx, 11, 45, 54

M
Manchuria, 9, 41, 50, 65
Manchu language division, 5, 6
Manchu people, 6, 41, 51, 58, 65
Mergen Bamba, 50, 54
Michael, Henry N., ix, 63, 69, 71
Mongolia, 12
Morgan, Jason, ix, 10, 11, 13, 15, 71

N

Nagishkin, Dmitriy, ix, 3, 63, 71
Nanays, 1, 5, 6, 40, 41, 50, 51, 52, 54, 58
Nani language group, 5
Negidals, 1, 5, 41
Nerchinsk Treaty, 2
Nikans, 41, 50, 51, 52
Nivkhi, ix, 1, 5, 6, 41, 66

O

oblast, 6, 65, 66
Olson, Wallace M., ix, xiii, 71
Orochi, ix, 1, 5, 6, 41
Oroks, 1, 5, 6, 41

P

Paleoasiatic, 6, 66
Pavlishin, Gennadiy, ix, 71
Planet Earth, xiii, 61
Polar bear, xii, xiii
Price, Robert, ix
Primorye *Kray*, 6, 9
Puninga, 29, 30, 31, 33, 34, 36, 37

R

Ramel, Gordon J.L., 14, 15, 71
raven, xi, xiii
rayon, 6, 65, 66
Ruddy, William, ix
Russian Far East, ix, 1, 2, 3, 6, 8, 9, 11, 12, 65, 71

S

sea lion, 54
seal, 15, 43, 54
Siberian tiger, ix, xii, 2, 9, 15
shaman, xi, 8, 43, 52, 54, 55, 66
shamanism, xi, 69
Slama, Brad, ix
snow leopard, 54
Soldiga, 29, 30, 31, 36, 37
Solomdiga, 17, 18, 19, 21, 28
sven, 8, 30, 66

T

taiga, 6, 19, 30, 31, 33, 37, 45, 47, 48, 52, 55, 61, 66
tiger, ix, xi–xiii, 1, 2, 9–15, 18, 21, 22, 28, 30, 31, 33, 39, 41, 43, 44, 45, 47, 54, 64, 71
Treadwell, Mead, ix
Tungus, 5, 8, 66
Tungusic language division, 5, 6
Tunguso-Manchu language branch, 5, 6

U

Udegeys, 1, 5, 33, 4-0, 41, 44
Ulchi, ix, 1, 5, 6, 41
Uralo-Altaic language family, 5, 6

W

walrus, 54
Weld, Luke, ix
Wixman, Ronald, 6
whale, xii, xiii
wolf, xiii

Y

yasak, 50, 51, 66
yukola, 40, 66
yurta, 33, 34, 37, 43, 44, 45, 66

Z

Zipes, Jack, xii, 63